Medieval and Tudor Needlecraft

Knights and Ladies in 1/12 Scale

Medieval and Tudor Needlecraft

Knights and Ladies in 1/12 Scale

Sandra Whitehead

First published 2002
by Guild of Master Craftsman Publications Ltd,
166 High Street, Lewes,
East Sussex, BN7 1XN

ISBN 1 86108 259 2

A catalogue record of this book is available from the British Library.

Cover and book design by Tim Mayer, Mayermedia
Cover and finished project photography by Anthony Bailey, Guild of Master Craftsmen
Photographic Studio
Illustrations by John Yates

Picture credits
Many thanks to the following for supplying material and giving copyright permission
to use their images in this book:

Detail of Mss. 6 f.125v (scarlet campion) used throughout this book was supplied by kind permission
of the Dean and Chapter of York: © Dean and Chapter of York.
Bridgeman Art Library, pages 47, 63, 82, 129 and 137;
British Library Manuscripts Department, page 53;
English Heritage Photo Library, page 105;
Eve Harwood, page 35;
R J L Smith & Associates, Much Wenlock, Shropshire, page 110;
Brian Davis, photographer and copyright holder and Geoff Sadler,
author of *Chesterfield: History & Guide* (Tempus Publishing), page 112;
Israel Museum, Jerusalem, title page and page 39.

Typefaces: Grail Light, Aquiline and Adobe Garamond
Colour origination by Viscan Graphics (Singapore)
Printed and bound by Kyodo Printing (Singapore) under the supervision of MRM Graphics,
Winslow, Buckinghamshire, UK

Contents

Introduction

It never ceases to amaze me, this wonderful world of miniatures. Almost everything we use in our everyday lives, both past and present, is available in miniature today. Nothing is sacred – if it can be made, it can be made in miniature.

For a designer, the world of miniatures is like a dream come true; it opens up a whole new world in which to explore and give form to one's imagination and fantasies, and develop one's artistic talents. The inspiration for developing a new project is very individual and reflects the unique nature of one's personality, lifestyle, interests and desires.

I first began collecting miniatures following a visit to a major dolls' house and miniatures show. I had never seen anything quite like it. The variety and quality of the craftsmanship astounded me and I just couldn't leave the show without purchasing at least one miniature. Of course, the one miniature turned out to be rather large: a six-roomed, Tudor-style dolls' house – perhaps a little ambitious for a beginner!

Having taken my purchase home, I stared at it in awe for a few weeks, mulling over the possibilities. I am passionate about historical accuracy, and details that didn't seem to quite fit the period began to leap out at me – the doors were not quite right for a Tudor home and neither was the door furniture – so I began to change little bits here and there.

Once I had altered the house to how I wanted it, I set about furnishing the rooms. I thought about making the furniture myself, but woodwork is not my strong point – and anyway, I'd already seen the items I wanted at the show, of course. The Tudor furniture was dark and heavy and needed a little softening, and the rooms needed to be a little more inviting. Tudor homes would have had plenty of needlework items – and these were projects that I could manage for myself. I tackled the project with enthusiasm, feeling rather like a designer for a film set, imagining the characters that might people the house. At the time I was engrossed in a series of wonderful books called *The Game of Kings* by the late writer Dorothy Dunnett, who is by far my favourite historical novelist. Her attention to detail is remarkable and I found myself visualizing the central characters as personalities for my Tudor house. So, another of my passions found its way into my miniature world.

Very soon, my wall hanging designs began to be greatly admired, so I gathered the patterns together along with their historical sources, and put them into my first book, *Celtic, Medieval and Tudor Wall Hangings in 1/12 Scale Needlework* (also published by GMC Publications) and my embroidery design business Knight Time Miniatures was born.

Since then, my life has become increasingly hectic, designing new needlepoint items for the dolls' house fairs, researching and developing new needlecraft ideas, giving talks about my work – as well as keeping up with my children, who insist that their miniature requirements are also met in full! Fortunately, as well as being my biggest critics, the children are my biggest fans, too.

The patterns included in this book are partly the result of requests by my readers for more wall hanging designs, and partly to demonstrate some diverse additional skills that are part of making miniature soft furnishings and costume, for example: cutting and making items from fabric, miniature knitting, costume design, embroidery, needlepoint and furniture upholstery. There are so many exciting

techniques to help you achieve your dreams of authentic-looking period items. As far as possible, the patterns are ordered by relative complexity – but to some degree this depends on your own experience at stitching needlepoint and making up costumes, so you may wish to use the book more flexibly and move backwards and forwards through the projects.

And for those stitchers who would like to work in alternative scales, the needlework designs can easily be reduced or enlarged to suit. The charts for some of the designs in this book feature the finished size at various scales. The real beauty of charted designs is their versatility; they can be used as wall hangings for the dolls' house, adapted for carpet and screen designs or framed as full-scale pieces to display in your own home.

The medieval and Tudor periods were full of drama and change, providing lots of inspiration for creating imaginative needlepoint costumes and furnishings for the dolls' house. And, whatever your experience of miniature soft furnishings and costume, I hope the projects featured here will inspire your own explorations into other miniature worlds beyond the realms of this book.

Have lots of fun!

Sandra Whitehead

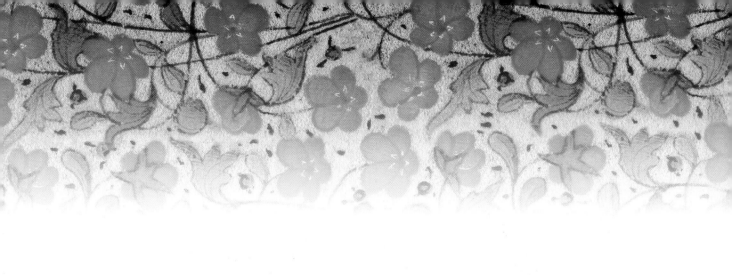

Getting Started

Working in Miniature

Working in miniature, whatever the scale, is very different to working full-scale items. Because everything is much smaller and more intricate, you must consider things like your eyesight and your posture. Ensuring that you work in a safe, comfortable environment is very important.

Your working environment

Before you begin work on your projects, it is important that you create a comfortable and well-lit environment. A chair to support your back while you work is a must, as is a good source of natural light for daytime working. If you work in the evenings or the available light is poor, special daylight or halogen bulbs are readily available so that you can continue to work without interruption. I also find some kind of magnification aid useful (see page 11 for more details). Even if you do use magnification aids, you should always exercise your eyes by altering your field of vision at frequent intervals.

If you are choosing thread colours, this task is best done in daylight as the colours look different under artificial light. Although a good light source is necessary for your stitching, very bright daylight shining directly onto the fabric makes the colours look very washed out, making it almost as bad as artificial lighting for colour selection. A slightly shady spot surrounded by good light is my personal preference for sewing. A further warning on daylight: never leave your threads or your work in strong sunlight as the sun bleaches the colour from the threads, leaving them faded and patchy; always keep them covered when not in use, or have a dedicated storage box to keep them in.

Miniature dos and don'ts

With miniature projects there are some guidelines to help you get the best from your work. I return to some of these in more detail in the following chapters, but it is worth keeping these things in mind from the beginning.

- **Patience is the key; work slowly and carefully and never rush a project or take short cuts.**

- **Maintain a clean, tidy work area and be organized.**

- **Make sure you wash your hands regularly. They need to be as clean as possible to avoid soiling your work.**

- **Do work in natural daylight when possible or use a good alternative source of light such as a lamp fitted with a daylight or halogen bulb.**

- **Do use magnification aids if necessary. Eye strain is a common problem when working with miniatures. The worst thing for a miniaturist is to incur a problem with his or her eyesight.**

Maintaining a safe and comfortable work station with good lighting is very important.

Materials and Equipment

Needlepoint designs

Threads

The threads used in this book are from the DMC stranded cotton range. I have also provided the Anchor and Madeira stranded cotton equivalent shade references with each of the designs in case you require an alternative thread or prefer to work with those brands.

Each thread contains six strands of cotton. The strands are slightly twisted together to form the thread. I have used two strands of the divisible thread throughout the designs. Use thread lengths of no more than 14–16in (35–40cm) at a time and then re-thread. This helps to avoid the friction that produces a 'fluffy' appearance on the surface of your work and thins the thread as you sew. After cutting your length of thread, separate out the six strands from each other and then put them back together in pairs ready to use.

A selection of materials and equipment required to create your needlepoint designs.

Fabrics and canvases

Fabric used for needlework has what is known as a thread count. The higher the thread count, the more stitches there are per inch (or 2.5cm) of the design. This is normally expressed as *tpi* (threads per inch).

22-count canvas is an evenweave canvas suitable for dolls' house projects, and is easy to work, though it is prone to distortion and is best worked on an embroidery frame while you complete the stitching. Evenweave means that the holes in the fabric are spaced at equal vertical and horizontal intervals which is important when working regular or diagonal tent stitch. As its name suggests, 22-count canvas has 22 stitches to the inch (2.5cm). This is sometimes expressed as *hpi* (holes per inch). The higher the hpi, the finer the fabric and the more stitches per inch.

After working your piece, the canvas may need to be blocked. Blocking is the technique used to remove or minimize any distortion of the canvas during stitching, and forms the piece back into shape ready for finishing (see page 28 for further details).

The majority of the needlepoint designs are worked on a 32-count evenweave fabric. Murano or 32-count Lugana are particularly suitable. If you have difficulty obtaining any of these canvases or fabrics, please check the mail-order suppliers at the back of this book (see page 146).

Needles

Tapestry needles are used for needlepoint. These have round or blunt tips so that they pass easily through the holes in the fabric without catching. They also have good-sized eyes to make threading easy. It is crucial that you use the best needle for the fabric or canvas you are working on, so that the pieces do not become distorted. The best size of tapestry needle for the 32-count projects is 26, while 24 is the better size needle for 22- and 24-count canvas.

I suggest that you have a number of needles available in your chosen size when you begin a project; it is useful to have some needles pre-threaded and ready for use rather than having to thread and re-thread a single needle.

Needle threader

The size 26 tapestry needle does require careful threading when using two strands of thread, so you may find that a needle threader is a useful addition to your range of equipment.

Frames

While it is not essential to sew the 32-count projects on a tapestry frame, I find that it is much easier to count threads when fabrics are mounted. Using a frame also means that the fabric is handled less, reducing the possibility of soiling. If you choose to use a frame, first edge the fabric with masking tape before mounting it onto the frame to help prevent the fabric from fraying.

Bar frames are also quite useful. They are widely available in packs and can be assembled into nine different-sized rectangular frames, ideal for mounting your projects. Bar frames are also available as individual pairs of sides so that you can assemble them to any size you require, and some are specially designed for miniature pieces. When using bar frames, though, do take care to ensure that they remain square, otherwise the canvas will distort. It is sometimes helpful to use a small table frame when you need to have both hands free.

Hoops are suitable for use on some of the finer fabrics such as linens but, if you use one, make sure that you remove it from the work every time you finish a session of stitching, so that it doesn't stretch the fabric or leave a mark. Use a hoop that's large enough to surround the whole stitching area, so that you don't ever have to tighten it over stitched areas. To help protect the fabric, the hoop can be covered with a strip of fabric or bias binding tape – or position a piece of tissue paper between the fabric and the hoop, tearing away the section of tissue paper that lies over the stitching area.

When using canvas, I never stitch it on a hoop or tambour frame as I find that the distortion is far greater than on the tapestry frame. Canvases such as 22-count petit point (or tent stitch) canvas or 24-count Congress cloth must be attached to a frame as they distort much more easily than the 32-count evenweave fabrics.

Scissors

A pair of sharp-pointed embroidery scissors is essential for the projects in this book. Make sure the embroidery scissors cut right up to the point of the blade to avoid fraying the threads. You will also need a pair of dressmaking scissors for cutting out fabric.

Avoid using either of these scissors for cutting out your paper patterns and cardboard templates; always keep a pair of general household scissors in your tool box for this purpose as this kind of work can blunt your sharp scissors and make them less efficient.

Magnification

Because of the nature of miniaturist work, it is almost always essential to use some kind of magnification aid to assist your work. Working on fine fabrics with small stitches for any length of time can cause eye strain. Many magnifiers are quite expensive (though the most expensive are not necessarily the best), but it is definitely worth the investment as good magnification and a decent light source are essential.

There are many different types of magnifier available on the market, some of which usefully combine a lamp and magnifier. Others have lights built into them, and some clip onto spectacles. Some magnifiers have an extra-strong section built into the main lens; it looks rather like a bubble of raised glass. This small lens is more powerful than the main lens and is useful for examining small areas of work in greater detail, and for threading your needle.

My favourite magnifier is a lens attached to a headband (see the photo on page 8). This has several advantages over alternative magnifiers; it is lightweight and comfortable and I can wear it over my spectacles. It is also portable and I don't have to keep taking it off when I want to refocus my eyes at a distance. It is amazing how much of a nuisance that can be! The lens is interchangeable too, enabling me to use lenses of varying strengths for different miniature tasks. If I need an additional light source, I use a small, adjustable floor lamp with a daylight bulb.

Laying tools

Laying tools are optional accessories that I find very useful for both needlepoint and cross stitch. A laying tool is placed under the thread while working so that the strands remain smooth and untwisted to give a better finish to the work. It is a blunt-ended implement, similar in shape to a long, large tapestry needle, and is used when more than one strand of thread needs to be worked together.

Laying tools are available from needlework shops and suppliers, and come in various shapes and sizes. Some are made of metal, others of wood or plastic, and some are finer than others, according to the type of thread being used: a fine one is most suitable for these projects. The tool that I use fits comfortably on my finger, but others are held in the palm of the hand. Mine looks like a half-ring with a metal cocktail stick attached (see below).

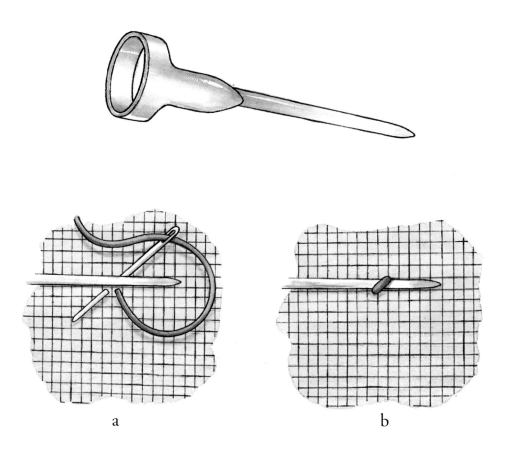

a   b

Stitchers use laying tools in different ways to suit their own working practices. I place mine on the middle finger of my left hand: I bring the stitch up through the fabric and, before I go back down through the fabric, I place the laying tool on top of the canvas where the stitch is to be worked. I then work my stitching thread over the projection (a) so that the thread can be straightened and untwisted before the tool is removed and the stitch completed (b). The threads lie much more neatly if you use a laying tool, and it really doesn't slow you down significantly. Unfortunately, I can only use this method when I have both hands free – that is, when my stitching is supported by a table frame or floor stand.

Stitching the costume designs

Working with miniature materials

There are some differences between making costumes for dolls in 1/12 scale and outfits for larger dolls. Because the fabric used to make miniature costume is not available in 1/12 scale thickness, you must use exactly the same fabric as for larger pieces. This inevitably means some limitations on the fabrics you can use. Only the most delicate velvets, linens, cottons, silks and minute patterned prints are suitable for 1/12 scale. There are specialist companies dealing with dolls' house fabrics and haberdashery and I recommend you try them (see page 146). In the medieval and Tudor periods, only natural fabrics would have been available, so authenticity also constrains your choice of costume materials.

A common problem when you begin designing and making miniature costumes is hemming. It is difficult enough to make fabrics drape attractively at this scale without distorting the garment further with a bulky hem.

Rather than resort to hemming, then, many miniaturists make use of narrow braid trimmings, fabric glues and anti-fraying agents when finishing costumes. Frayed seam edges in 1/12 scale are impossible to handle: the tiniest amount of fraying can ruin a seam. It is quite acceptable to use glue to secure trimmings to garments at this scale.

Most sewing for miniature costume is by hand. A sewing machine is useful for larger seams, but is otherwise rather cumbersome. I tend to use a sewing machine for tiny embroidery trimmings – not for assembling miniature outfits. Sometimes you will experience problems with fitting the costume to your doll because of the period style of the garment, but this can be overcome with careful assembly.

Dolls and doll kits

1/12 scale dolls can be commissioned from doll makers or specialist miniature shops, and there are a number of different kinds of dolls available, depending on your needs – from those you make yourself in kit form to ready assembled and wigged dolls.

Many doll makers accept commissions for specific requirements to suit the period. The feet, for example, can be made with or without shoes, and the shoes can be heeled, high-heeled or flat. The dolls' faces can be painted with open or closed eyes. Dolls can be made to sit or stand. Some bodies are made of porcelain and in a fixed position, while some are strung so that the joints are manipulable. Some dolls have a soft flexible body and porcelain arms, legs and head, while there are dolls now available with ball-and-socket joints so that they can be posed. These are ready made for you to dress or can be supplied in kit form with full assembly instructions.

Some dolls are sculpted from modelling compounds – polymer clays such as Fimo and Sculpey. If you have the time and patience, have a try at sculpting your own character figures. Some wonderful characters can be created. An inspiring guide to making your own is *1/12 Scale Character Figures for the Dolls' House* by James Carrington (see page 147 for further details).

Fabrics

The projects in this book make use of natural fabrics such as silk, fine wool, very thin leather, linen, printed cottons, cotton lawn and muslin. If you use patterned fabrics, make sure they are sympathetic to the period in question; they should not be contemporary prints. Fine, stretchy cotton fabrics are useful for making tights and leggings for dolls. For some of the Tudor projects, use handmade lace;

lace trimmings were popular in this period (see page 146 for suppliers, or consult a miniature lace maker – many can be found at dolls' house fairs). General haberdashers simply do not have the same range as the specialist suppliers and it is worth being selective about your choice of fabrics.

A selection of brightly coloured period fabrics, braids and trimmings.

Braids and trimmings

These need to be very fine and you will probably need a specialist supplier for these, too, as widely available commercial braids are almost all too wide and thick for our use. The widest braids that I use are about ½in (1.25cm) and these are too wide for most of the projects and only suitable for use as fringing or upholstery trimming. Most of the braid and trimming that I use is less than ¼in (0.75cm).

Fabric glues and glue syringes

These are readily available. Tacky glues are the best for miniatures. They dry clear and take enough time to bond to allow you to reposition a braid or trimming if necessary. Use a glue syringe to apply glue as the amount required is often tiny and must be applied accurately. I use a glue syringe with a long, thin nozzle. The glue is quite thick and the nozzle is very fine, so in order to ensure the glue runs freely, stand the tip of the nozzle in a small amount of warm water as you work. Be careful: some fabrics – silk, in particular – can be stained by badly applied glue. The tacky glue is also suitable for assembling dolls from doll kits and especially for attaching wigs.

Pleating aids

These are commercially available from dolls' house suppliers. They are usually made from a flexible, rubber-like material and have troughs and ridges through which fabric is pressed and dampened into shape. Once the fabric is dry, it is neatly pleated and holds its shape very effectively. Pleated fabrics are useful for bed and window curtains, skirts and trimmings, and can also be used to make perfect ruffs for Tudor dolls. The pleaters come in various sizes to suit different projects; a fine pleater is very useful for the projects in this book (see page 35 for techniques).

Rotary cutters and scissors

General purpose scissors are required for cutting out the patterns, and a good pair of sharp scissors is needed for the fabric cutting. You could use dressmaking shears for the fabric, but I find them rather too unwieldy to cut patterns accurately. I also keep to hand a small pair of embroidery scissors.

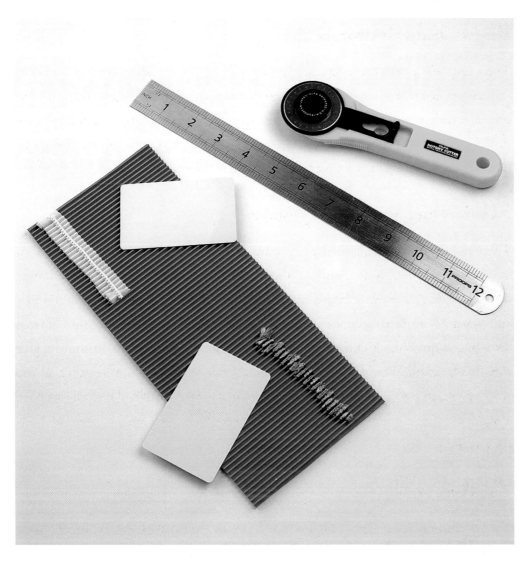

The pleating aid, metal-edged ruler and rotary cutter are invaluable tools for producing perfect 1/12 scale costumes and soft furnishings.

For cutting leather and fine strips of fabric, a rotary cutter is very useful. To use this effectively you need a cutting mat and a steel rule. Use rotary cutters with care; they are incredibly sharp. For safe storage, they are fitted with a cutting guard.

Tweezers

A pair of tweezers is very useful for wigging and many other functions, for example turning out small items of clothing such as sleeves to the right side after seaming, and for accurately positioning braids and trims.

Beads and jewellery findings

These are very useful for miniature projects. My supplier has a lovely selection of Celtic-style jewellery findings that could be used at 1/12 scale. I use them for the medieval lady costume featured in this book (see page 68) and also for hanging rods. Beads and findings are available by mail order, and suppliers can often be found at dolls' house fairs. For more details on suppliers, see page 146.

Mohair and viscose

These materials are hair substitutes used for doll wigging. Both are available in a range of shades and quantities. Only small quantities are required to wig a single doll. Mohair and viscose are both available from suppliers (again, see page 146) and dolls' house fairs. Wigs can also be bought ready made from some suppliers. If you can't find the style of wig that you require, please ask your supplier as many will make one to order.

Paints

Porcelain dolls can have their period shoes painted directly onto the feet using enamel or acrylic paints. You can also paint facial features or hair (if you wish to avoid the wigging process).

Leather

Shoes can be made from small amounts of very soft leather, for example glove leather. Leather can be purchased in small quantities and in many shades from dolls' house accessory suppliers.

Stitching and Finishing Techniques

Stitching the needlepoint designs

The needlepoint projects are all stitched on 32-count evenweave fabric with the exception of the Lovers in the Garden tapestry and the two settle cushions (see pages 52 and 98 respectively). For the former, if you want to reproduce this design as a cushion cover, you should use 14-count Aida. The tapestry is stitched on 24-count Congress cloth and the settle cushions onto 22-count canvas. If you change the size of any of the designs by using a lower or higher count fabric you will also need to make adjustments to the quantity of thread required. Depending on the fabric count, you will require a fewer or greater number of strands, and will need to adjust the size of your canvas and your tapestry needle accordingly. For very fine fabrics, use a beading needle. These can be cut to suitable lengths and the point re-ground to form a tapestry needle-like blunt end.

I always allow at least 2in (50mm) of extra fabric around the design area to allow for finishing the design. If the piece is to be framed as a picture, I suggest that you leave at least 3in (75mm) of unworked fabric around the design area.

Most of the projects use only a small quantity of fabric and threads – making most projects a relatively inexpensive venture – and many suppliers will obligingly sell them in small quantities, too.

Preparing the fabric

Thread counting is the one thing that many stitchers fear the most with charted designs. It is easy to be just one stitch out when sewing in miniature. If you have a recurring motif on the border, a single stitch can make a big difference to the finished design. It is not quite as obvious as it would be on a large design, but you will know it's there!

First, centre the design on the fabric. Do this by folding the fabric or canvas into four so that you can mark the centre point (see (a) and (b) on the diagrams below). Some people like to stitch a contrasting guide thread down the centre lines (c) to help them count the squares and stitches, or you could mark out the lines with a fading marker pen. The lines fade after about 24 hours, so you may need to mark them again. You can also insert a pin gently at the centre point (d). Alternatively, run a line of small tacking or running stitches along every tenth thread in a strongly contrasting colour to make a grid on the fabric which you can easily pull out afterwards. Personally, I don't find I need to do this, but if you are inexperienced, this approach may give you extra confidence.

Next, cover the edges of the fabric with masking tape. This helps to prevent the edges of the fabric – particularly non-interlock canvas – from fraying, and stops thread from catching on the edges of the stiffer mono canvas. It provides a secure base through which to attach the design to a frame.

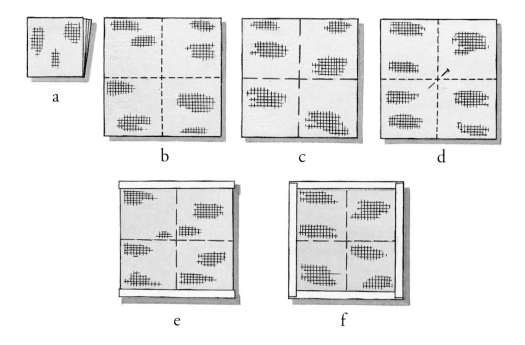

Getting ready to sew

Cut lengths of each colour of your chosen threads to approximately 16in (40cm). Separate each strand from the thread and then rejoin the strands in pairs. Each thread has six strands, so you will have three lengths of double strand thickness from each 16in (40cm) thread of stranded cotton. As you sew, the threads will naturally start to twist together again. If you allow this to persist, you will notice that as the twist tightens, the threads seem to become thinner. To prevent this happening, allow the thread to hang down from the work with the needle dangling at its end; the weight of the needle untwists the thread. Alternatively, use a laying tool to help lay the threads neatly and smoothly.

Position your chart where you can see it clearly. (You may wish to use the black and white chart which can be photocopied and enlarged.) Some stitchers like to mark off their worked stitches with a highlighter pen as they sew; this reduces the risk of mistakes in counted-thread sewing, and you can still see the worked stitches through the colour of the highlighter if you need to rework an area.

The stitches

The designs in this book are stitched using two different methods of producing a diagonal needlepoint stitch. The two methods of stitching look the same from the front of the work, but quite different when you look at the back.

Tent stitch

Tent stitch is used to sew the detailed areas of the designs. Tent stitch seems particularly appropriate for stitching these designs, as Tudor embroiderers frequently used it for their work. It's also sometimes known as 'Continental' stitch.

Come up through the fabric at the odd numbers and down where there is an even number indicated, as shown below.

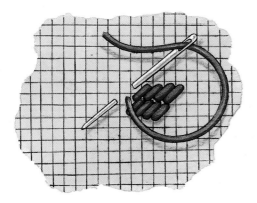 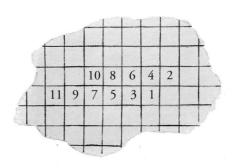

Diagonal tent stitch

This is also known as basketweave stitch because on the reverse side it resembles the interwoven lines of basketwork. It distorts the work slightly less than tent stitch, and is commonly used for stitching larger areas of the designs and for filling in the background.

Follow the basic stitching sequence shown in the diagrams below, working across the canvas in diagonal rows. Again, bring the needle up through the canvas at the odd numbers and back down through it at the even numbers.

If you are a cross stitcher, you will notice that both stitches resemble the half cross stitch that should be familiar to you. Don't be tempted to use half cross stitch instead of tent or diagonal tent stitch in these needlepoint designs; it doesn't cover the canvas so well, and it also has a much greater distorting effect on canvas.

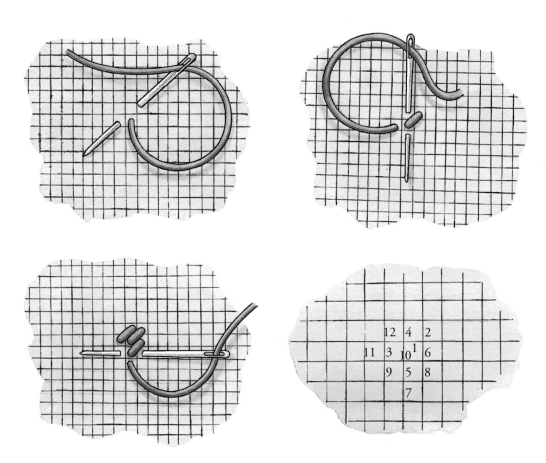

Putting in a single stitch

There will be occasions on some designs where you need to work a single stitch in a particular colour. (Additionally, it is easy to miss a single stitch and not notice the omission until later!) In both these instances, follow these guidelines to drop the odd stitch into place with little effort.

Using only a single strand of thread instead of the usual two, fold the thread in half and push the loop through the eye of your tapestry needle. Pull the thread so that the looped end is longer than the alternate end. Bring the needle up through the fabric and then down through the loop as you complete the stitch. The stitch is now fastened in place through the loop on the underside of your work and you will only have to sew in the remaining end of thread.

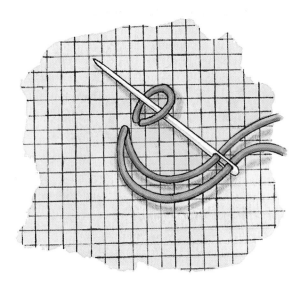

Wrong side of work

Beginning the design

Once the canvas is on a frame, the sewing is generally worked in an up-and-down motion through the canvas, as shown over the page. This is sometimes referred to as a 'stabbing' action.

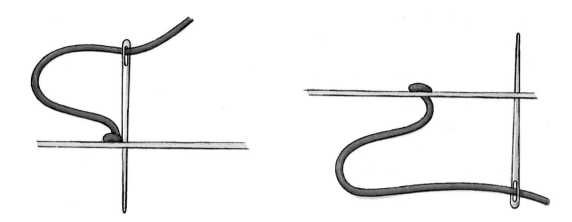

Starting a thread

Put a knot in the end of the thread. Starting in the middle of the design area (unless instructed otherwise), pass the needle from the front of the work to the back about six stitches away from the position of the first stitch and in the direction in which you intend to sew. The knot is now on the front of the work. Bring the thread up at the point you wish to make your first stitch, and sew towards the knot. When you reach the knot you can cut if off as close to your work as possible, taking great care not to cut into any of your worked stitches. The beginning of the thread is now anchored securely behind the worked stitches. Start any new threads in this way, making sure that each thread is anchored properly before cutting it off.

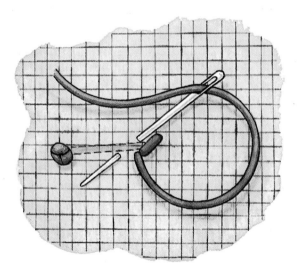

Finishing a thread

When you are coming to the end of a thread, pass the end through at least six stitches on the reverse of your piece of work and then any remaining thread can be cut away so that it looks tidy. The thread is better anchored if it's finished horizontally or vertically.

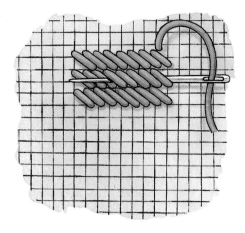

Order of stitching

The order in which you build up a stitched design is really a matter of personal preference. Many people recommend that the detailed areas of any design are stitched first and then the background. Any areas in white are usually stitched last as this helps prevent the thread from becoming marked while working; it also helps prevent the white thread from picking up tiny fibres of other colours as they are worked.

The order of working a design really depends on the design itself. If a picture has a plain border, the central design is worked first and then the border – if you do it the other way round, it is easy to miscount the number of stitches in a plain border which may mean that the central design will not fit properly.

If the border has a regular geometric pattern, then this is usually worked first so that you can see that it works out correctly; any miscounting of stitches in geometric designs is very obvious. For the same reason, it's best not to jump from area to area as you sew.

With some of the designs I recommend that the outlines of certain areas are worked first, and then filled in later. With each design I've given some guidance on a suggested stitching order, but as I've said, it's far better to sew in your own style than to try and change your sewing practice significantly. There are no rights and wrongs, only suggestions that may help.

Patchwork landscaping

This is a technique I have developed for my miniature embroideries to make an otherwise plain and rather uninspiring background come to life – particularly areas where you want to feature an outdoor landscape. I use a thread from the range of colours and create an outline which contains shades of different-coloured threads within it. For the Dragon Panel (see page 46), I used a variegated green thread which includes shades of green from very pale to mid-green to give the fields in the background a more authentic texture. I worked the background in diagonal tent stitch but, instead of working straight diagonal lines that would give the background a stripy appearance, I stitched random blocks diagonally.

To work this technique, cut several threads at once and use two strands from one, followed by two strands of another thread. This keeps the mix of colours random and prevents the repetition of shading. Next, work small, irregular-shaped areas in diagonal tent stitch, but don't allow the areas to become too large; it is better to work smaller patches. As you approach the foreground, allow the patches to increase in size to accommodate the perspective of the work and make the shading more realistic. For a landscape of heather, try purple and pink shades or mixed light blues to liven up a sky. Use a band of greens on the horizon in stronger shades to look like a forest.

The variegated green thread gives the fields in the background of the medieval dragon panel an authentic, patchy texture.

Following the charts

Each of the medieval and Tudor designs in this book has both a colour and a black and white chart; many people prefer to use the latter because they find that the symbols are easier to distinguish than blocks of colour. On both types of chart, one square represents one stitch (the squares do not represent squares of the canvas). If you're working with a colour chart, the colour key alongside it indicates the colour you should use in your needle for each stitch on the chart.

The black and white charts use symbols in the squares; the key alongside the chart indicates the thread colour that should be used for each stitch marked with that symbol on the chart. This is particularly useful where several shades of one colour are used in a single design, or design area. The black and white charts will also help you if you prefer to enlarge and photocopy a chart and mark off the stitches as you work them.

All the keys provide the shades of DMC stranded cotton required, plus the Anchor and Madeira equivalents. Alongside the references you will find a colour description for each thread; these are rough descriptions rather than definitive names and are included to help ensure you are using the correct range of colours for the project.

Remember, too, that the colours of available threads vary slightly from one manufacturer to another, so sometimes the equivalent given for a particular colour may be the closest match rather than an exact duplicate. This can be a significant disadvantage if you choose to use threads from a different manufacturer; if possible, I recommend you use as many as possible from one range of threads.

Sometimes, if there is no exact match for a particular colour in the new range, the manufacturer may give a near equivalent. This may result in the same shade being substituted for two (or more) colours in your original design. If this does happen, just choose a suitable alternative shade from the range available, or substitute your own colour choice.

Finishing

Once your stitching is complete, remove the design from the frame. If the piece has no distortion and the corners are still at true right angles (if appropriate), you can omit the blocking process. In practice, canvases are rarely true anyway.

Cleaning

Sometimes, as we work, oils from our hands can be deposited on the fabric which, with age, can cause discolouration. If this happens, evenweave fabric can be washed gently by hand. If you do wash the piece, make sure that it is laid flat and in its original shape as it dries to avoid distortion in the fabric.

Canvas should not be washed unless absolutely essential as the sizing compound will be removed from the canvas, leaving the fabric soft and floppy. However, it can be dry-cleaned.

Blocking

Blocking is the technique used to restore a piece of needlework to its correct shape if it has distorted during work. It is very easy to distort a piece of canvas. It is stiffened with an ingredient that softens when handled. As soon as this softening occurs, the piece readily stretches out of shape. (That's why using a frame while you stitch minimizes distortion, as it reduces the handling of the fabric.) Signs of stretching are unlikely to be evenly distributed across the canvas, so some areas may become more out of shape than others.

The blocking process uses a small amount of moisture to 're-size' the canvas. The damp canvas is pinned to a blocking board that is marked with straight lines; the edges of the fabric can be eased out straight and then pinned in position. You can easily make a blocking board at home or, alternatively, use any piece of board into which you can insert drawing pins (thumbtacks) and something with a right angle, such as a set square or an old picture frame.

To prepare the canvas for blocking, dampen it by steaming thoroughly. Do be careful, as steam can produce a nasty scald. A steam iron can be used for this, or you can hold the fabric over boiling water (wearing rubber gloves to avoid the skin getting in contact with the steam). Don't let the fabric get too wet. The dressing on the canvas needs to be dampened, to loosen the weave, but if you make it too wet the dressing is simply flushed out of the canvas altogether.

Pin the canvas to your board, right side up, while it's still warm and damp, using the lines on the board or the corners of your right angle to help you get the sides and corners of the finished work straight. (If you're using something wooden for your right angle, take care – wet wood may stain your work.)

Leave the canvas until it's completely dry, then you can remove it from the board for finishing.

If a canvas is very distorted, it can still be restored to its original shape. Use the blocking board and, after steaming the canvas, place it on top of a clean cloth with the worked design face down on the board. (Use a cloth which will not transfer colour to your design!) Pin the canvas to shape (face down), then gently rub thin wallpaper paste into the reverse of the design with your fingers, and leave the piece to dry for a few days. I've never needed to use this method myself when I've used a frame for working the designs, as the frame prevents the canvas from distorting too severely, but I'm told that it works a treat.

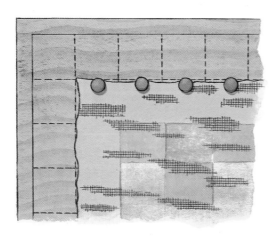
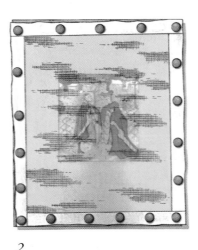

1 *2*

1 If you have a blocking board, use drawing pins to secure the damp stitching to the board as
shown. The lines on the board are guides to keep the work straight.
2 You can use any rigid frame to block your stitching – even an old picture frame works well.

Framing

Some designs can look wonderful framed. The only framed design in this book is the Lovers in the Garden tapestry (see right and page 52), which looks really effective. It's generally recommended that you shouldn't cover needlepoint with glass, because it is a technique appreciated for its texture as well as its looks, but this tapestry is in regular, tiny needlepoint stitches and can be covered with glass to help protect it from dust and dirt.

Using a frame to display your tapestry protects it from damage.

Making up wall hangings

Once you have blocked your piece of work, cut a piece of cotton or calico backing fabric to the same size as the canvas, adding a little extra allowance all round to make a small hem. Fold under the hem and lightly press it.

Select a coordinating braid or ribbon to make the tabs to hang the tapestry. Decide how many you would like, cut the ribbon or braid into lengths of 2½in (6cm) (a), and fold each tab in half (b). Using slip stitches, fasten each tab at even intervals (c) to the reverse side of the upper edge of your canvas.

Materials
Fray Stop glue

PVA glue

Glue syringe

Cotton backing fabric

Braid or coordinating ribbon
(for the tabs)

Dowelling, two beads and wood stain
(for hanging rod, optional)

Sewing cotton in matching colour
to backing fabric

Sewing needle

Fold under a single hem around the edge of the backing fabric, and press. The backing piece should be slightly smaller than the front of the wall hanging. With wrong sides together, slip stitch the backing piece to the reverse of the canvas, covering the places where the tabs are attached (d).

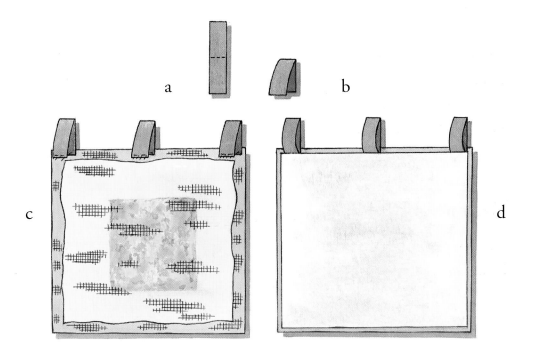

a

b

c

d

If you want the wall hanging to lie flat, use a layer of double-sided bonding web between the canvas and the backing fabric, or use a single-sided lightweight iron-on interfacing in place of the backing fabric. If you do this, be careful not to distort the canvas by over-ironing it.

To display, make a hanging rod for the wall hanging from a length of very fine wooden dowelling and secure the beads with glue to either end of the dowelling to decorate. (You may find that you need to pare down the very ends of the dowelling to fit the beads.) Alternatively, ready-made hanging rods are available from suppliers (see page 146 for details).

Making up chair cushions

Remove the stitched design from its frame and block it, if necessary. Glue a narrow line of Fray Stop around the outer edge of the design, avoiding the stitched area, and allow the glue to dry.

Cut out the design leaving at least ¾in (2cm) excess fabric around the border. Fold the excess under and press. Whether you would like your cushion to have rounded or square corners, cut out a template from thin, white cardboard to the shape of your chair seat. Use the template to cut out a shape from thin felt.

Place a small amount of wadding in the cushion, then stick the felt shape to the base of the cushion. Trim the join around the edge of the design and the felt base with narrow braid.

Materials
Cardboard template
Piece of thin felt
Length of narrow braid trimming
PVA glue
Glue syringe
Small piece of wadding

Making up a bedspread

Remove the design from the frame and, if necessary, block the work with the right side down. Glue a line of Fray Stop around the outer edge of the design and allow this to dry.

Cut out the design leaving an excess of ½in (1.25cm). Using the design as a

Materials
Fine cotton fabric (for the lining)
Coordinating sewing thread
Sewing needle
Fray Stop glue
Glue syringe

template, cut the shape of the design out of thin cotton fabric. With right sides together, stitch the lining to the bedspread panel around the outer edge of the design and as close to the stitching line as possible. This can be done either by hand or on a sewing machine. Leave an area of the seam unstitched so that the bedspread can be turned through to the right side. Sew up the opening using slip stitch.

Fit the bedspread onto the bed. A good tip for moulding the bedspread to the shape of the bed is to wrap both together in cling film for a few days. Once removed, the bedspread stays miraculously in place, draping over the edge of the bed.

Making up table carpets

Remove the stitched table carpet design from the frame and block the design, if necessary. Glue a ½in (1.25cm) line of Fray Stop around the outer edge of the panel, avoiding the stitched area, and allow the glue to dry.

Cut the panel from the fabric leaving an excess of at least ½in (1.25cm) around the design. Make a cardboard template for the top of the

Materials
Thin felt

Fray Stop glue

PVA glue

Glue syringe

Piece of thin, white cardboard (for the template)

Narrow braid edging (optional)

Sewing thread

Sewing needle

table and use this to cut out a matching shape from your piece of thin felt. Trim the edges of the felt very slightly to just marginally smaller than the finished design. Fold the hem under the panel and use a little glue to secure in place. Stick the felt backing to the reverse of the panel, covering the hem.

If desired, edge the panel with a very narrow braid. A good idea, too, if you want to secure the table carpet properly, is to use some PVA glue to mount the panel to the table top.

Making up settle cushions

Remove the completed design from the frame and block, if necessary. Glue a thin line of Fray Stop around the outer edge of the design, avoiding the stitched area, and allow the glue to dry.

Cut out the design, leaving a ½in (1.5cm) hem of excess fabric around the design. Fold it under to make a hem and lightly press. Using the design as a template, cut out two identical pieces from the fine cotton.

Materials
Fray Stop glue

Glue syringe

Narrow length of picot braid

Backing fabric in cotton or fine velvet
(in coordinating shade)

Sewing needle and thread

Wadding (or)

Small plastic beads (or)

Fine agricultural sand or rice
(for the filling)

Piece of fine cotton fabric
(to make an inner bag for the filling)

With right sides together, stitch around the outer edges of the bag, leaving a small area of the seam unstitched so that the pillowcase can be turned through to the right side. Stuff the inner case until quite full with the filling, but do not overstuff it so that it remains fairly flat. Sew the opening closed and place the bag onto the worked design.

Cut another piece of fabric, slightly larger than the cushion design, to make a backing for the cushion. A lightweight velvet is particularly good for this. Turn a small hem and slip stitch the backing to the design area with the inner cushion sandwiched between the design and the backing fabric.

To display, place the cushion on the settle. The rice, plastic pellets or fine agricultural sand filling enables the cushion to be realistically shaped. A prod here and there gives the cushion a 'sat upon' look.

Pleating fabric and hair

A pleater is a flat, rectangular piece of rubber segmented into grooves into which fabric or hair (for wigging the dolls) is formed into pleats. The pleaters are available in several pleat widths depending on how fine you require them to be. The larger pleaters are used for making pleated upholstery items, soft furnishings and curtains for dolls' houses, the smaller ones for pleating fabric for dolls' clothes and hair.

1

2

1 Working in the pleats with the pusher.
2 Roll away the pleater rather than the fabric when removing the piece of pleating.

To make a ruff for your Tudor dolls, cut a section of cotton lawn approximately 6 x 3in (150 x 60mm) in size, and fold this in half along the long side. Dampen the fabric and then, using the pusher – which resembles a credit card – press the fabric into the grooves of the pleater. Once complete, leave the fabric to dry. Before removing the fabric from the pleater, glue a length of white picot braid down the length of the centre of pleated fabric. Leave this to dry and then remove the pleated fabric from the pleater. The braid will help to hold the fabric which you should now cut to the correct size for the neckline of your costume to form an erect ruff.

To make pleated, wavy hair, first dampen the mohair or viscose hair and then push it into the grooves of the pleater, as before. Next, push it in alternate directions to give it a more natural appearance. Once dry, the wavy hair can be used to wig your doll.

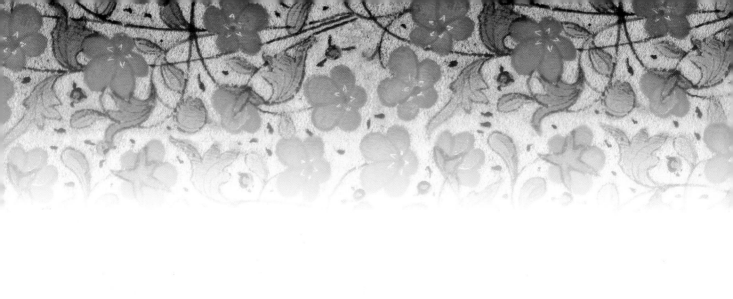

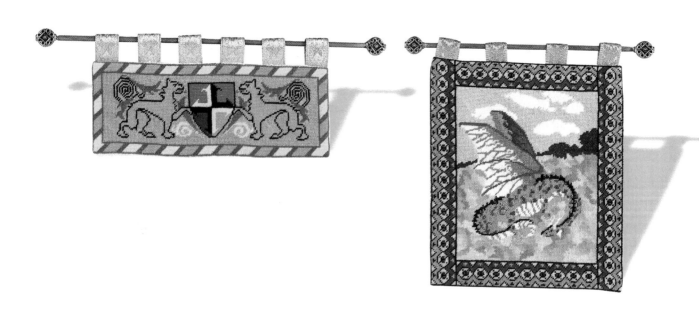

Medieval Designs

he Rabbit Panel

This delightful panel is inspired by a charming rabbit motif that features in an illuminated manuscript, held in the collection of the Israel Museum in Jerusalem. The original manuscript features a twin rabbit motif, which is slightly different, but I was really attracted to this little fellow.

Working in miniature

This panel is suitable for both medieval and Tudor periods. I've taken the medieval-style panel and added a curling leaf motif rather than flowers to the background in keeping with the natural motifs of the period. This easy design took me only a few hours to complete. It is easily adaptable to other items such as chair and settle cushions by using a higher count fabric or, alternatively, to make a larger version into a framed picture. The design can also be used to practise 60-count gauze work. Don't forget to adjust the fabric, threads and needles according to the fabric count.

Detail of rabbit motif taken from the Rothschild Miscellany housed in the collection of the Israel Museum in Jerusalem.

Materials

32-count Murano (Lugana),
6in (15cm) square

Small tapestry frame

Masking tape

Tapestry needle, size 24 or 26

Pair of small embroidery scissors

Needle threader (optional)

Magnifier (optional)

Stranded cotton threads,
1 skein of each colour

Stitch count

62 × 74

Design size (excluding tabs)

1¾ × 2¼in (4.4 × 5.9cm)

Alternative scales

Count	Design size
14-count	4⁹⁄₁₆ × 5¼in (11.2 × 13.4cm)
24-count	2½ × 3in (6.6 × 7.8cm)
48-count	1⁵⁄₁₆ × 1¾in (3.3 × 3.9cm)
60-count	1 × 1¼in (2.6 × 3.1cm)

Method

1 Edge the fabric with masking tape and mount it to a small tapestry frame.

2 Using your preferred method, centre the design on the fabric (see page 20). This design has a very simple border so it doesn't matter if you work this or the central design first.

3 Work the detailed areas in tent stitch and the background in diagonal tent stitch.

4 For finishing techniques, see pages 30–31.

Thread key

Colour	DMC	Anchor	Madeira		Colour	DMC	Anchor	Madeira
Deep dusky rose	223	895	0812		Mink	840	1084	1912
Light delphinium	312	979	1005		Deep chestnut brown	898	359	2006
Umber	435	365	2010		Light green	988	241	1402
Pale toffee	738	942	2013		Straw	3047	852	2205
Deep cranberry	815	44	0513		Deep sage green	3051	269	1508
Deep navy blue	823	152	1008					

Thread key

	Colour	DMC	Anchor	Madeira		Colour	DMC	Anchor	Madeira
▬▬▬▬	Deep dusky rose	223	895	0812	■■■■	Mink	840	1084	1912
♡♡♡♡	Light delphinium	312	979	1005	▽▽▽▽	Deep chestnut brown	898	359	2006
♡♡♡♡	Umber	435	365	2010	⁄⁄⁄⁄	Light green	988	241	1402
▢▢▢▢	Pale toffee	738	942	2013	★★★★	Straw	3047	852	2205
◤◤◤◤	Deep cranberry	815	44	0513	⬡⬡⬡	Deep sage green	3051	269	1508
●●●●	Deep navy blue	823	152	1008					

The Lion and Shield Panel

Based on an authentic thirteenth-century wall decoration, this popular heraldic panel of the period can also be found in books of decorative ancient motifs. For me, it seems to represent heroic qualities such as strength and honour, and is a beautifully simple execution of its kind.

Working in miniature

This makes a great feature for a half-panelled room in a Tudor mansion or castle, as the design fits nicely above the panelling. It is relatively simple and shouldn't take you long to complete. If you stitch the design onto a coloured rather than plain fabric, you can omit the background if you wish, but I much prefer to work the background to retain the tapestry effect.

Materials

32-count Murano (Lugana),
11 x 7in (28 x 17.7cm) in cream

Tapestry frame

Masking tape

Tapestry needle, size 24 or 26

Pair of small embroidery scissors

Needle threader (optional)

Magnifier (optional)

Stranded cotton threads,
1 skein of each colour

Stitch count

212 × 64

Design size (excluding tabs)

6⅞ × 2in (16.8 × 5.1cm)

Alternative scales

Count	Design size
14-count	15 × 4½in (38.5 × 11.6cm)
24-count	8¾ × 2¾in (22.4 × 6.8cm)
48-count	4½ × 1¼in (11.2 × 3.4cm)
60-count	3½ × 1in (9 × 2.7cm)

Method

1 Edge your chosen fabric with masking tape and mount it to the tapestry frame.

2 Using your preferred method, centre the design on your fabric (see page 20).

3 Complete the design using two strands of stranded cotton throughout. Work the border design in tent stitch and diagonal tent stitch and then the detail of the central panel. Fill in the central panel and the background areas using diagonal tent stitch where necessary.

4 Because of the length of the panel, it is best mounted as a wall hanging in a dolls' house or miniature castle (see pages 30–31 for further information on finishing techniques).

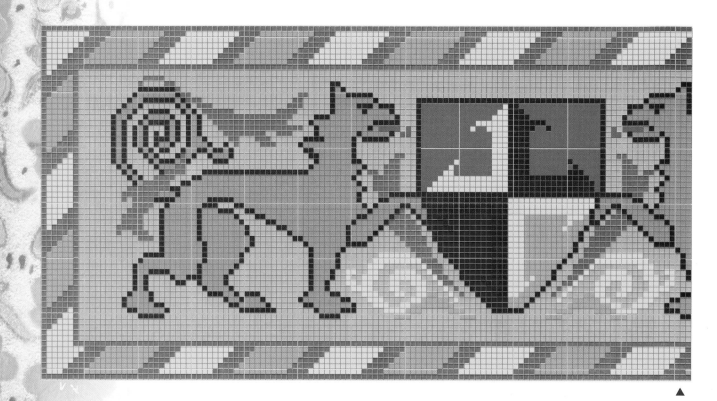

Thread key

	Colour	DMC	Anchor	Madeira
	Deep scarlet	349	1098	0212
	Deep buff	612	853	2108
	Dark yellow ochre	680	901	2210
	Dark blue green	699	230	1303
	Dark primrose	725	305	0108
	Copper	922	1003	0310
	Deep sage green	3051	269	1508
	Dark chocolate	3371	382	2004

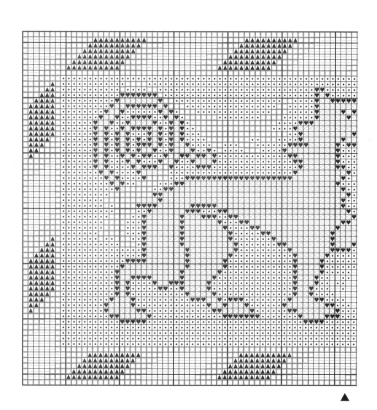

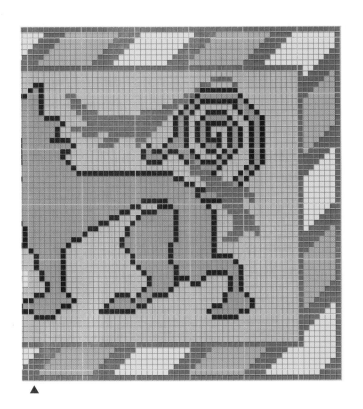

Thread key

Colour	DMC	Anchor	Madeira
Deep scarlet	349	1098	0212
Deep buff	612	853	2108
Dark yellow ochre	680	901	2210
Dark blue green	699	230	1303
Dark primrose	725	305	0108
Copper	922	1003	0310
Deep sage green	3051	269	1508
Dark chocolate	3371	382	2004

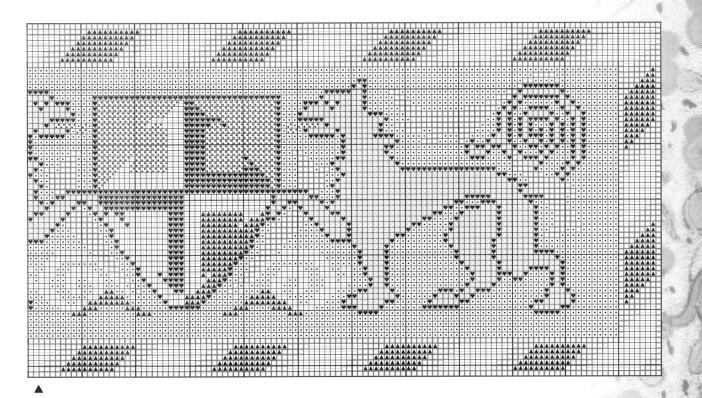

Dragon Panel

Of all the mythical beasts, it is perhaps the dragon that endures most vividly in our imaginations. While in some cultures the dragon is conceived as a friendly, amenable beast, it is more often represented as a fire-breathing symbol of horror.

In Christian texts, it is often used to depict Satan, its scaly body equated with that of the serpent in the Garden of Eden. In Christian societies, the slaying of the dragon was once a powerful symbol of humankind overcoming evil and heresy. Our best example of this is St George, the patron saint of England and of soldiers, who is frequently depicted as a knight battling with a ferocious dragon.

The war-like Vikings adorned their war ships with the image of the dragon, appropriated as a symbol of power. Celtic dragons commonly feature on medieval manuscripts, and the dragon appears on the jewellery of the Anglo-Saxons, too.

In ancient China, the dragon became a symbol of the might of the emperors, and of fertility. It is also one of the symbols of the Chinese zodiac.

The dragon is also used as an heraldic sign and is frequently depicted in art and architecture. Modern theories suggest that the dragons of ancient English folklore may have some foundation in fact; that the dragon may have evolved from dinosaurs. Fact or fiction, we have an enduring fascination with this fantastical beast.

Depiction of George and the dragon taken from the Flemish Book of Hours, *probably Bruges (c.1500–05), held in the Fitzwilliam Museum, University of Cambridge.*

Materials

32-count Lugana (Murano), 12in (30cm) square

Tapestry frame, 12in (30cm)

Masking tape

Tapestry needle, size 24 or 26

Pair of small embroidery scissors

Stitch count

160 × 171

Design size

5 × 5⅜in (12.7 × 13.6cm)

Alternative scales

Count	Design size
14-count	11½ × 12¼in (29 × 31cm)
24-count	6¾ × 7⅛in (16.9 × 18.1cm)
48-count	3¼ × 3½in (8.5 × 9cm)
60-count	2¾ × 2⅞in (6.8 × 7.2cm)

Working in miniature

The dragon panel is worked in a more contemporary style than the period, and might easily be adapted from a wall hanging into a framed picture. The dragon is depicted lying in wait for a victim, or perhaps a battling knight – although I have been told that it looks as though it has just crash-landed!

I like to make these panels as simple as possible to sew, but this sometimes means that the background looks a little plain. By using a variegated thread in several shades of green, and sewing the grass in the background in irregular patches, the overall effect is much more rugged. I call this stitch technique patchwork landscaping (see page 26 for instructions). It works very well on miniature pieces!

Thread key

Colour	DMC	Anchor	Madeira
Light delphinium	312	979	1005
Dark almond green	319	1044	1313
Almond green	320	215	1311
Donkey grey	451	233	1808
Grey mint green	503	875	1702
Light ocean blue	597	1064	1110
Pale toffee	738	942	2013
Deep cranberry	815	44	0513
Deep navy blue	823	152	1008
Deep sage green	*3051	269	1508
Powder blue	3755	140	1013
Blanc	White	2	White

Note

* If you want to try the patchwork landscape technique, substitute 3051 with DMC 94 (Anchor 1216), olive green ombre.

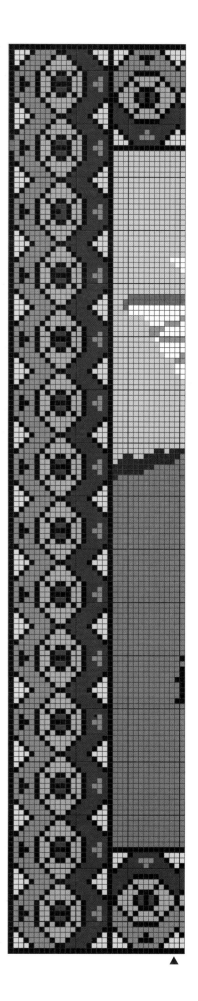

Method

1 You can use either a round (tambour) or embroidery frame for this design. Edge the fabric with masking tape before mounting it to the frame.

2 Centre your design on the canvas.

3 Thread your needle with two strands of cotton less than 14in (35cm). A size 24 needle is best for this.

4 Work the design in tent stitch throughout. Work the detail of the border pattern first and then fill in the background as follows: the tree skyline section of the pattern using the worked border pattern as a guide, then the outline of the dragon wings, then the dark blue ridge along the dragon's back (which will help with the placement of the dragon's body, neck and head). Finally, fill in the detail on the dragon, followed by the clouds, sky and grass.

5 Once complete, finish the piece (see pages 30–31).

Thread key

	Colour	DMC	Anchor	Madeira
◁◁◁◁	Light delphinium	312	979	1005
৪৪৪৪	Dark almond green	319	1044	1313
////	Almond green	320	215	1311
∴∴∴	Donkey grey	451	233	1808
∘∘∘∘	Grey mint green	503	875	1702
▪▪▪▪	Light ocean blue	597	1064	1110
⦂⦂⦂⦂	Pale toffee	738	942	2013
┝┝┝┝	Deep cranberry	815	44	0513
▷▷▷▷	Deep navy blue	823	152	1008
✶✶✶✶	Deep sage green	*3051	269	1508
	Powder blue	3755	140	1013
☐☐☐☐	Blanc	White	2	White

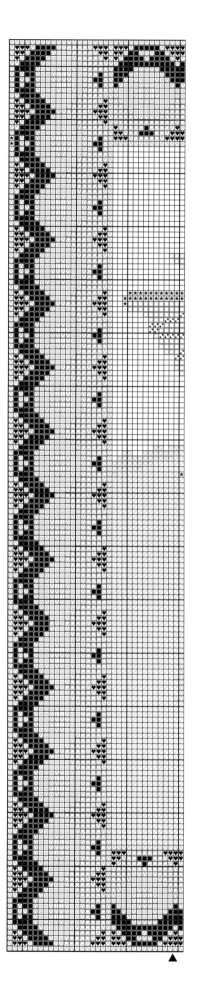

Lovers in the Garden Tapestry

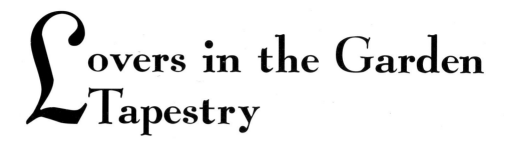

Christine de Pisan was an extraordinary woman of her period. Born in 1363, she was married at fifteen to twenty-four year old Etienne de Castel. It was clearly a match based on love – they adored each other and lived very happily with their daughter and two sons. But, at the age of thirty-four, Etienne was obliged to accompany King Charles VI to Beauvais when he suddenly took ill and died, leaving Christine with the considerable burden of three small children, her mother and a niece, two younger brothers, and a large household to support. In addition, Etienne's financial affairs were found to be in chaos.

Frontispiece from Christine de Pisan's Book of 100 Ballades *held in the collection of the British Library Manuscripts Department.*

The comfortable lifestyle promised to Christine was no longer secure. Worse, there were very few options open to her – remarriage was a possibility, but she loved Etienne so passionately that she had vowed never to wed another. Instead, she turned to writing and became Europe's first professional woman writer. From this body of work we learn the extent of the love she felt for her family and the struggles she faced after Etienne's death.

By the time she died in 1429, Christine de Pisan had established a brilliant literary career. The frontispiece of her *Book of 100 Ballades* features a charming depiction of a lover and his lady. I like to think that it represents Christine and her husband, Etienne.

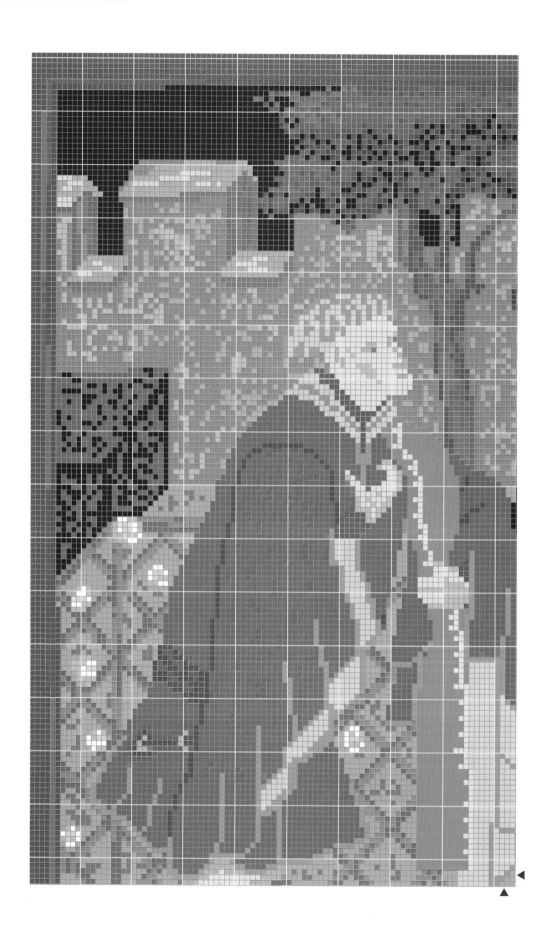

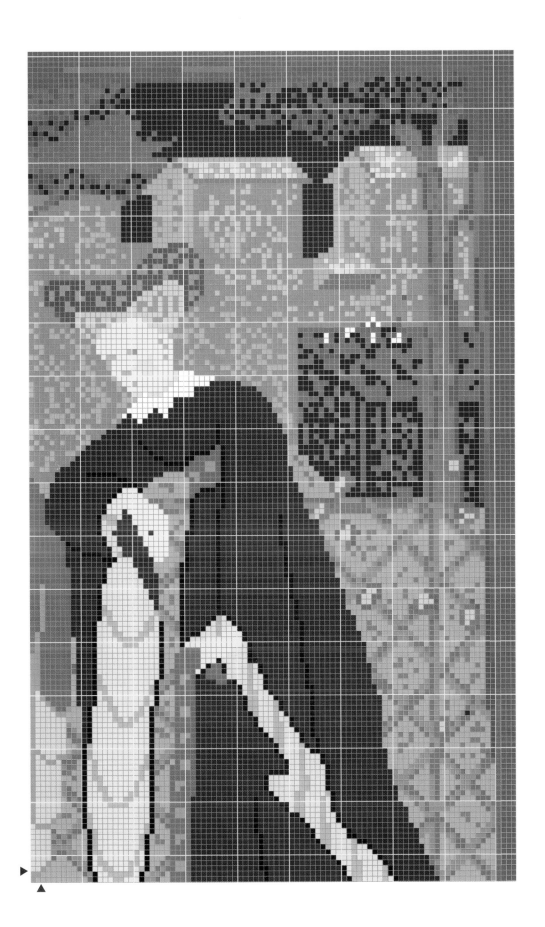

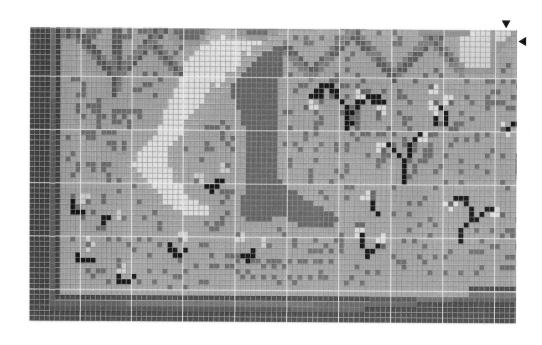

Thread key

Colour		DMC	Anchor	Madeira		Colour		DMC	Anchor	Madeira
	Deep dusky rose	223	895	0812			Deep navy blue	823	152	1008
	Pale rose	225	271	0814			Green sand	832	945	2202
	Dark grey	317	400	1714			Mink	840	1084	1912
	Dark almond green	319	1044	1313			Dark warm grey	844	1041	1810
	Deep rust red	355	1014	0401			Very dark peppermint	909	230	1302
	Steel grey	414	235	1801			Flesh	945	881	2313
	Light grey	415	398	1803			Medium straw	3046	887	2206
	Donkey grey	451	233	1808			Sage green (2 skeins)	3052	859	1509
	Light donkey grey	452	232	1807			Medium grey green	3363	281	1602
	Greengage	581	280	1609			Brick red	3772	1007	0812
	Dark green grey	645	8581*	1811			Pale coffee	3864	376	0313
	Deep ash grey	646	8581*	1812			Rust red (2 skeins)	3830	5975	0402
	Ash grey	647	1040	1813			Dark dusty rose	3858	896	0811
	Dark yellow ochre	680	901	2210			White	Blanc	2	White
	Dark flax blue (2 skeins)	792	941	0905						

Note

* These Anchor conversions give the same colour reference.
Substitute one of these for Anchor 393, deep stone grey.

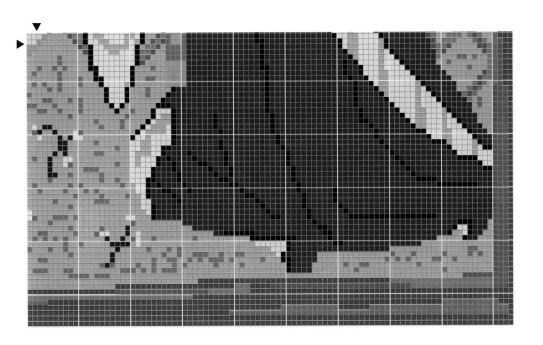

Materials

32-count fabric Congress,
12in (30cm) square, cream

Tapestry frame

Pair of embroidery scissors

Tapestry needle, size 24

Masking tape

Magnifier (optional)

Cotton backing fabric, cream

Matching sewing thread

Sewing needle

Braid (for the tabs)

Hanging rod, dolls' house curtain
pole or similar item (for mounting)

Stranded cotton threads,
1 or 2 skeins of each colour

Stitch count

184 × 207

Design size

5¾ × 6½in (14.6 × 16.4cm)

Alternative scales

Count	Design size
14-count	12¾ × 14¾in (33.4 × 37.6cm)
22-count	8½ × 9½in (21.2 × 23.9cm)
48-count	3¾ × 4¼in (9.7 × 11cm)
60-count	3 × 3½in (8.1 × 8.8cm)

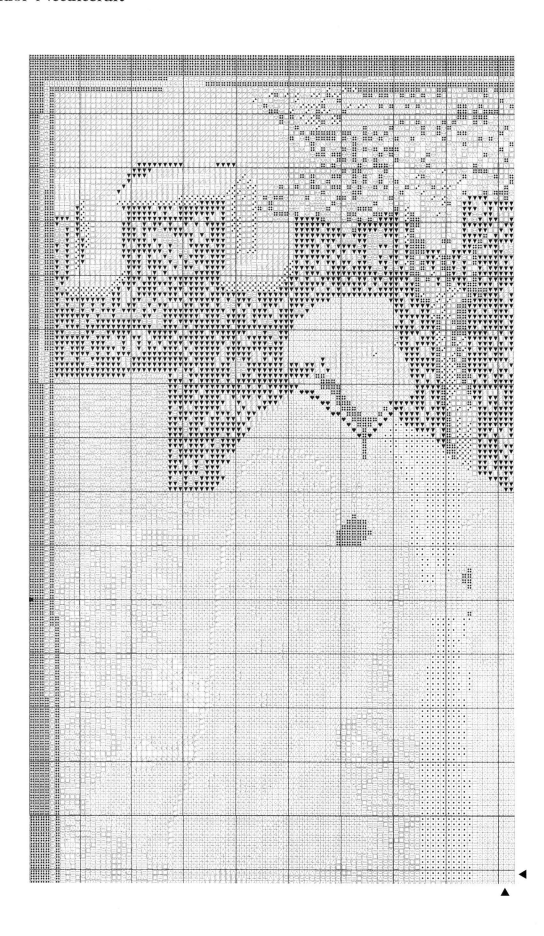

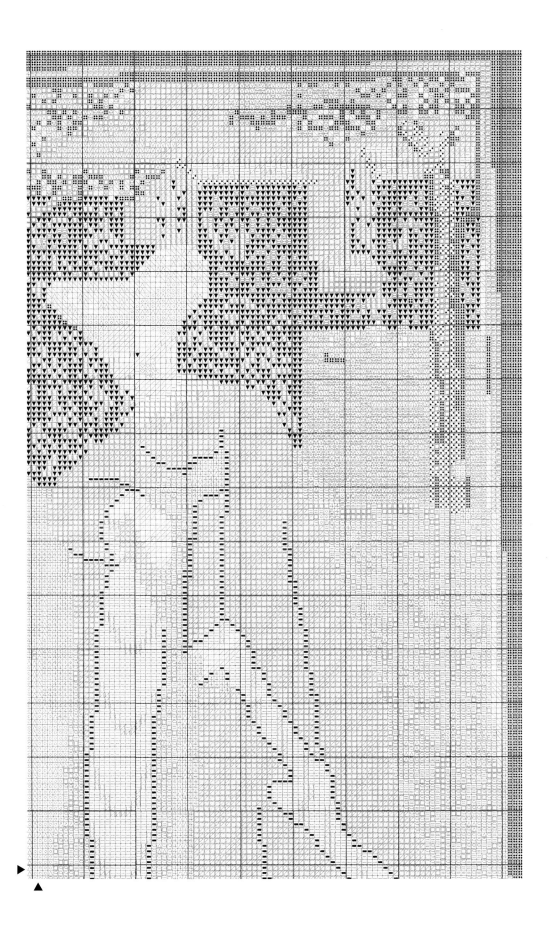

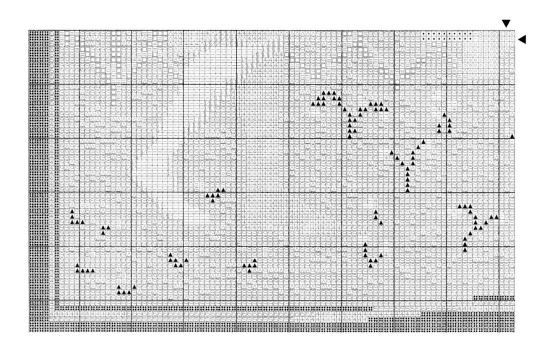

Thread key

	Colour	DMC	Anchor	Madeira		Colour	DMC	Anchor	Madeira
:::::	Deep dusky rose	223	895	0812	====	Deep navy blue	823	152	1008
/////	Pale rose	225	271	0814	∧∧∧∧	Green sand	832	945	2202
▢▢▢▢	Dark grey	317	400	1714	⋗⋗⋗⋗	Mink	840	1084	1912
▲▲▲▲	Dark almond green	319	1044	1313	\\\\	Dark warm grey	844	1041	1810
⋉⋉⋉⋉	Deep rust red	355	1014	0401	◔◔◔◔	Very dark peppermint	909	230	1302
≡≡≡≡	Steel grey	414	235	1801	♡♡♡♡	Flesh	945	881	2313
----	Light grey	415	398	1803	○○○○	Medium straw	3046	887	2206
▼▼▼▼	Donkey grey	451	233	1808	⊊⊊⊊⊊	Sage green (2 skeins)	3052	859	1509
◓◓◓◓	Light donkey grey	452	232	1807	▽▽▽▽	Medium grey green	3363	281	1602
△△△△	Greengage	581	280	1609	⟨⟨⟨⟨	Brick red	3772	1007	0812
▦▦▦▦	Dark green grey	645	8581*	1811	∈∈∈∈	Pale coffee	3864	376	0313
⬡⬡⬡⬡	Deep ash grey	646	8581*	1812	4444	Rust red (2 skeins)	3830	5975	0402
⋈⋈⋈⋈	Ash grey	647	1040	1813	⊑⊑⊑⊑	Dark dusty rose	3858	896	0811
♥♥♥♥	Dark yellow ochre	680	901	2210	⊐⊐⊐⊐	White	Blanc	2	White
▽▽▽▽	Dark flax blue (2 skeins)	792	941	0905					

Note

* These Anchor conversions give the same colour reference. Substitute one of these for Anchor 393, deep stone grey.

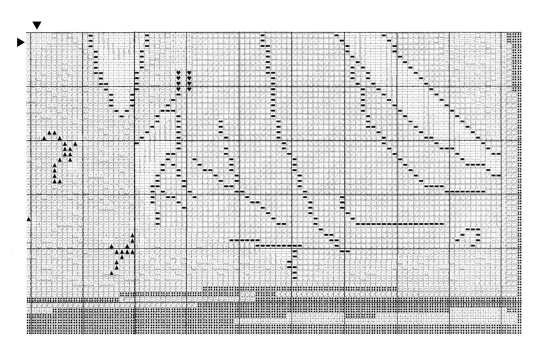

Method

1 Edge the canvas with masking tape in the normal way and mount it to the tapestry frame.

2 Centre the design on the canvas.

3 Thread your needle with two strands of stranded cotton and begin to sew your piece, working in tent stitch and diagonal tent stitch where necessary, and starting at the top right-hand edge of the canvas. Diagonal tent stitch is generally used to work large blocks of a single colour; there are just a few areas which require this stitch, as most are more detailed and shaded.

4 Once complete, mount and frame your work (see pages 28–30 for further details).

Horse in Caparison

The tournament was a very important part of life for a medieval knight. It enabled young knights to practise handling their horses and weapons in readiness for real combat. It was also the forum where experienced knights could display their skills and attract the attention of nobility to secure an offer of employment. Considerable sums of money could be won – and lost – at the tournaments. Defeated knights often lost their armour, weapons and horses to their victorious opponents. The tournament was also sometimes organized to settle disputes.

As time passed, the tournament became more about entertainment than confrontation. While blunted weapons became commonplace, the risks were still real and many knights sustained serious – or even fatal – injury.

Jousting knights on horses in caparison from Sir Thomas Holmes' Book, *c.1445, English school (15th century), held in the British Library, London.*

The horse's caparison was extremely well-decorated to proclaim the rider's identity clearly. Shields, surcoats and horses' caparisons featured the knights' coat of arms which added to the sense of pageantry.

Working in miniature

This horse caparison is really easy to make. The only difficulty is ensuring the pattern fits your 1/12 scale horse. The little sewing that is involved is easy to do by hand.

Materials

Two pieces of 12 x 10in (30 x 25cm) fabric
(I used cotton and slubbed silk) in contrasting colours

Pair of dressmaking scissors

Pair of embroidery scissors

Two lengths of matching braids:
one very fine length, 3yd (2.75m) long
and another ¼in (0.6cm) wide and 2yd (1.75m) long

Length of fringed trim, 20in (0.5m)

Tacky glue

Fray Stop glue

Two sheets of A4 paper or thin card

Pair of scissors

Drawing pencil

Ruler

Method

1 First, to make your pattern, place the miniature horse on its side on an A4 sheet of paper or thin card and draw an outline around it. Compare its shape to the pattern pieces and make any necessary adjustments in the dimensions. Cut out your pattern and then the shape into two along the line marked A to B.

2 Begin with cutting out the pieces for the hind drape. Cut out pattern pieces (ii) and (iv) from the slubbed silk. The edges of slubbed silk tend to fray, so once cut out, use Fray Stop along the edges.

3 Turn pattern piece (ii) over and cut out one piece in the patterned cotton. Next, cut out two diamonds from pattern (v) in patterned

cotton, and one pattern piece (vi) in patterned cotton. When using cotton with a distinctive design, make sure the direction of the print remains the same for all pieces. For the drape, you should end up with the left-hand side in gold slubbed silk and the right-hand side in patterned cotton.

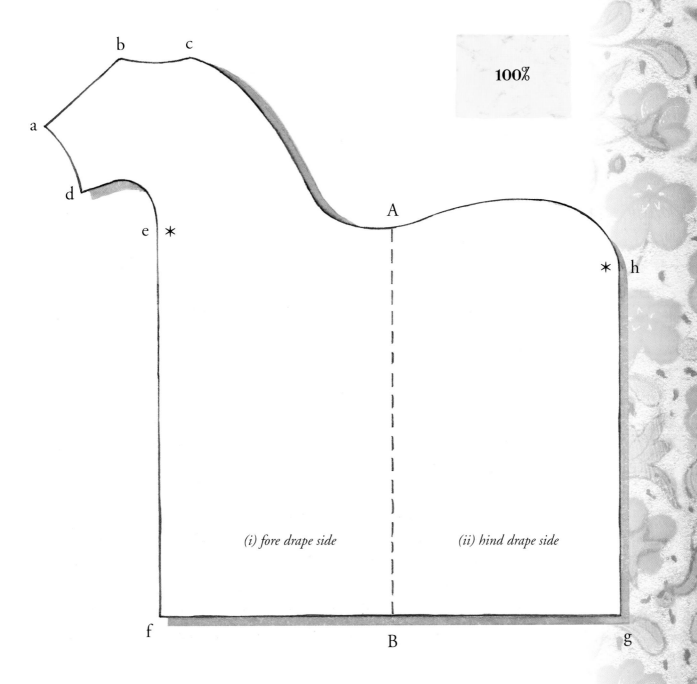

100%

(i) fore drape side

(ii) hind drape side

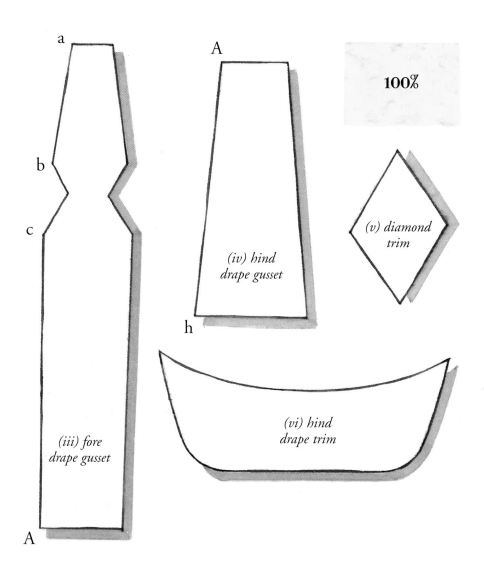

a

b

c

(iii) fore
drape gusset

A

A

(iv) hind
drape gusset

h

100%

(v) diamond
trim

(vi) hind
drape trim

4 Insert the hind drape gusset between the two pieces of hind drape
from A to (h). With the right side upwards, trim both back seams
with a length of the narrow braid. On the wrong side, edge all raw
edges from B on one side of the drape to B over the back gusset at A
on each side and down to B at the other side of the drape. Also, trim
from (g) at the lower edge of the hind drape to (g) on the other side.
Trim the lower edge from B to (g) on both lower edges with fringed
braid and the inside edge of B to (g) with the narrow braid. Edge the
raw edges of pattern piece (vi) with narrow braid inside and out and
then stick the ends of the piece across the back of the hind panel so
that the two halves are held loosely together below the horse's tail.

5 Next, work on the fore drape. This drape is easier to complete than it looks and only requires a little sewing. As above, use Fray Stop on the edges for the slubbed silk pieces. Cut out the pattern as follows: one piece from pattern (iii) in slubbed silk. Turn piece (i) over and cut out another piece of slubbed silk. Turn pattern piece (i) over and cut a piece from the patterned fabric. If you have cut these out correctly, each half of the front drape should be in the opposite colours to the hind drape.

6 Placing the front gusset piece between the two halves of the front drape, and with the wrong sides together, sew the seam from A to (c) on each side. Leave a gap in the seam for the ears (area (c) to (b)) and then sew from (b) to (a) on each side. Turn the drape to the right side and check its fit by slipping the fore drape over the horse's head. Trim around the inner part of the gap left at (b)(c) with narrow braid on each side of the drape and then trim from (a) through (b)(c) to A. Next, with the right sides uppermost, and using the wider braid, trim the edges from (d) to (f) on both sides of the fore drape, and also from B on the lower back part of the drape over the gusset area and down to B on the other side. In addition, trim the edge (d) on one side to (d) on the other side around the nose area of the drape with the narrow braid to cover any raw internal and external edges. Place the two diamond patterns, one above the other, on the slubbed silk side of the fore drape and use the narrow braid to trim them as you have on the hind drape. Trim the outside edges (b) to (f) with fringed braid. Fit the fore drape onto the horse and then slip stitch the drape from (d) to (e) to hold the drape under the horses' lower jaw and down the neck.

Finishing option

If you feel ambitious, paint a coat of arms onto the plain slubbed silk using silk paints instead of using the diamond-patterned fabric. All you need now is a knight – and an opponent!

Medieval Lady

This design is based on the ladies' fashions of the reign of Richard I (1189–99). They were very elegant with an emphasis on flowing lines and simple styling. Evidence suggests that the only undergarment that ladies wore was a simple chemise and that's all – so no panties! Made of very fine, soft wool, the robe (or kirtle) was considerably longer than the height of the wearer, with excess fabric secured around the waist, probably by a drawstring. A belt made of fabric, braid or leather was worn over this to disguise the gathered fabric at the waist. A tunic with deeply cut away sides, was worn over the kirtle.

Because medieval houses were not noted for their warmth, women often wore a mantle lined with the pelts of small, short-haired animals, too; it was draped over their shoulders and fastened by a strap across the front of the chest. Underneath their outer garments, they also wore a kind of loose-fitting cotton hose or stocking. Garments were more often than not quite plain; lengths of patterned braid were sometimes used to edge the neck and wrists of a garment. At this time, very little jewellery was worn either, with the exception of a brooch to fasten the neck of the robe.

By this time, crusaders returning from the Far East were bringing back with them silks and damasks. The availability of more colourful, luxurious fabrics such as cloth shot through with gold thread, was becoming more widely available – although this was really reserved for court dress.

Women's hair was worn in a caul or snood; something like a hair net, it fastened over the hair at the back of the neck. The hair was dressed either in long plaits, sometimes supplemented by the addition of false hair or coiled into a knot in the caul.

Working in miniature

It is quite difficult to find an appropriately draping fabric for 1/12 scale ladies' garments. I have used a printed cotton fabric trimmed with white braid for the kirtle, and a decorative length of braid for the girdle. I have attached Celtic-style jewellery findings to add weight to the end of the girdle and to help keep its shape. I used slubbed silk for the mantle which has enough weight for the garment to drape nicely. The headdress is made of fine white cotton lawn and fine cotton net with a little length of white braid.

Materials

1/12 scale female doll, with a flexible body and plaited hair

Fine wool, silk, or printed cotton, 12 x 10in (30 x 25cm)
(for the kirtle)

Piece of toning slubbed silk or very fine wool,
12 x 10in (30 x 25cm) (for the mantle)

Scrap of fine white cotton lawn (for the headdress)

Scrap of fine white cotton net (for the caul)

Fine braid trimming (for the sleeves, hem and neck of the kirtle)

Fine braid trimming in a matching shade
(for the edges of the mantle)

Jewellery findings (optional)

Tacky glue

Glue syringe

Small pair of sharp scissors

Cotton threads and sewing needle

Short lengths of fine and thicker braid
(for the kirtle hem and front neck)

Fray Stop glue

Double-sided lightweight bonding

Method

1 First make a paper pattern and check the fit of the garment on your
doll. Cut a sample outfit from kitchen roll and try this against your
doll to gauge the general fit of the garment, but mainly the length
of the kirtle, which should be overlong and have a small train at the
back. Make any necessary adjustments for your doll.

2 Using your chosen fabric for the kirtle, cut out one robe back and front. The kirtle should have very tight sleeves, but I have designed them a little wider so that the doll's hands fit through the cuffs of the sleeve. Make a small slit along the front of the neckline as indicated on the pattern, to ease the garment over the doll's head. Use Fray Stop along the edges of the fabric. Allow the glue to dry.

3 With the right sides of the fabric pieces together, and using a sewing machine with toning thread and a small stitch length, stitch along the shoulder and side seams of the kirtle. Alternatively, sew by hand. Make small snips along the curved seam from A to B to enable the seam to lie flat before turning the garment to its right side. Take care not to cut right up to the seam line.

4 Ease the dress onto the doll. Insert the doll's feet first through the neckline of the kirtle so that it is easy for the arms to fit into the sleeves. It is possible to use a porcelain doll but, if so, do take care when dressing it; you can slit a little more of the neck if necessary.

5 Using a very find braid, trim the neckline and sleeves on the right side of the fabric. Use a glue syringe with a fine nozzle to apply a thin line of glue to the fabric and allow it to dry before attaching the braid.

6 Use a thicker length of braid to cover the raw edge at the hem of the kirtle. Use the same braid to cover the neck slit.

7 Using a complementary thread and following the line, gather together the kirtle pieces at the waist of the doll. Pull the gathers close to the doll and fasten off.

8 Tie a length of patterned braid around the waist of the doll, and attach jewellery findings to the ends of the braid. To tightly secure the belt, sew it in place rather than knot it, which is a little bulky.

9 Cut one piece of the mantle pattern from your chosen fabric. Use Fray Stop on the cut edges and allow the glue to dry. If you are using silk, avoid using glue with too thin a consistency as this can bleed into the silk and mark it very badly.

10 Trim the raw edges, both inside and outside the mantle, with a narrow length of complementary braid glued carefully into place.

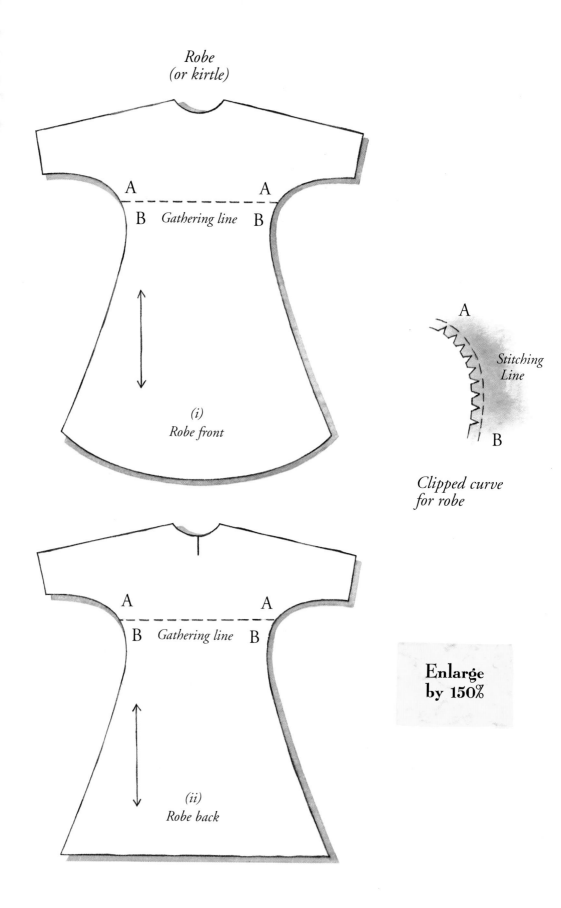

Robe
(or kirtle)

A   A

B   *Gathering line*   B

(i)
Robe front

A

*Stitching
Line*

B

Clipped curve
for robe

A   A

B   *Gathering line*   B

(ii)
Robe back

**Enlarge
by 150%**

Neck edge

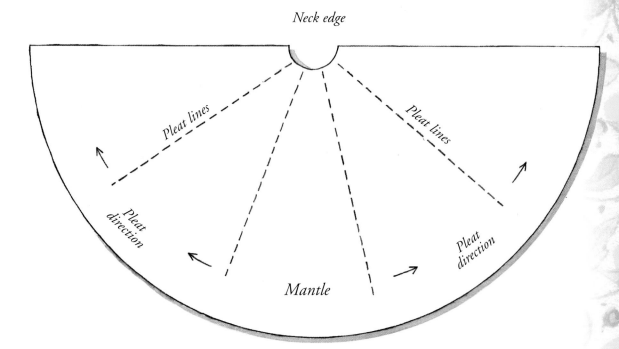

Pleat lines

Pleat lines

Pleat direction

Pleat direction

Mantle

Enlarge by 150%

Headdress

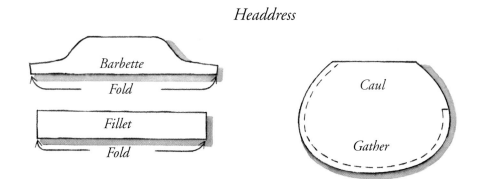

Barbette

Fold

Fillet

Fold

Caul

Gather

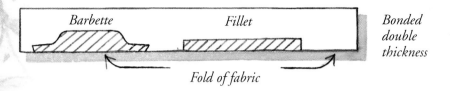

Fabric placement for barbette and fillet on bonded cotton lawn

100%

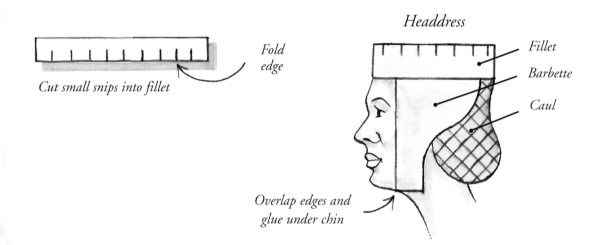

Fold edge

Cut small snips into fillet

Headdress

Fillet

Barbette

Caul

Overlap edges and glue under chin

11 Try the mantle on the doll. In order to make the fabric drape nicely, iron pleats into the fabric along the pleat lines. Place the mantle over the kirtle and glue into position on the shoulders and, if necessary, to the sleeves of the kirtle, to hold the front of the mantle in place. You can also use a little glue on the inside of the pleats at the lower end to hold the pleats in shape. If you find that the mantle still looks very stiff, wrap the doll tightly in cling film and leave for a day or two to help mould the mantle to the doll. Trim the mantle with small tassels or jewellery findings at the shoulders.

12 If you plan to wig your doll, you can do so now before making the headdress.

13 For the headdress, fold a small length of fine cotton lawn in two, and bond the two sides together using double-sided bonding fabric so that when you cut out the pattern you have a double thickness

of lawn. Place the pattern pieces for the barbette and fillet to the edge of the fold before cutting, so that you only have one edge that is not raw when the pattern is cut out.

14 Place the barbette onto the top of the doll's head and fold the narrow ends into place under the chin. Glue the ends together. Cut tiny snips about $\frac{1}{8}$ in (3–4mm) deep at intervals of $\frac{3}{16}$ in (5mm) along the folded edge of the fillet. This is the top edge of the fillet. Fasten the fillet around the head and over the sides of the barbette like a crown and glue into place at the back of the head.

15 Cut one piece of fine net using the caul pattern. Run a gathering thread around the caul at the curved edge. Put the plaits of hair into a neat coil at the base of the neck; you can stitch the coil into place if you prefer. Gather the caul and ease it into place over the coiled hair. Sew the top of the caul to the back of the fillet and disguise the seam with a tiny length of narrow braid.

Alternative design

Once you have made one medieval lady, you might like to try a slightly different design, this one rather more modest in style (below).

Court Jester

Most civilizations have a history of clowns, buffoons, fools or jesters. The latter term dates from the Tudor period – before this time they would have been called the king's or court fool. Many jesters were employed at court, but many nobles also retained their own household fools.

The fool – almost always male – is historically a unique figure in society with a contrary status. He had a very low social position, existing as a solitary, rather rootless figure who moved from one group to another at social functions, and eating separately from other members of the court. Yet he performed a service of considerable value in the community and enjoyed a special bond with his master. His primary role was to use humour to relieve his master from the tedium of court, household and state affairs.

The word 'fool' implies a simple-witted character, but this was by no means the case. Many fools were multi-talented – they were skilled minstrels, acrobats, jugglers and poets. Some were notable warriors. Many were very intelligent and exploited their role to improve their prospects. Having his master's ear, a successful fool could enjoy a position of relative power and be well-rewarded by his master but, like a slave, he relied absolutely on him for financial support which, if withdrawn, propelled him into obscurity and, most likely, poverty. The ambiguous character of the fool meant that he was frequently used as a spy – sometimes for the monarchy or nobility, and sometimes to undermine them. The fool could get away with the kind of behaviour prohibited to other members of society. Some had very long and respectable careers, spanning the reign of several monarchs during this period. Court jester James Lockwood, who was first employed by Henry VIII (1509–47), continued to work through the reign of Edward VI (1547–53), followed by Mary I (1553–58) and long into the reign of Elizabeth I (1558–1603).

The fool's attire altered considerably. The fools of Elizabeth's reign, for example, were required to dress as members of the court in doublet and hose, stockings and hats. Only the shocking colour combinations and additional decoration distinguished them from the other courtiers. Elizabeth I employed a female dwarf at court of whom she was particularly fond. She was not strictly a fool, but the favours heaped on her by Elizabeth indicate her great popularity. On the other hand, as a princess, Mary's female attendant Jane, who was employed by Mary's mother, Catherine Parr, was described in 1546 as 'the Queen's fool', so there may be some ambiguity over their role.

Working in miniature

The 1/12 scale fool in this project is in keeping with the medieval court jester. He is a jolly, rather portly, porcelain-bodied doll, holding a 'marotte' or 'poupette'. The latter is a child's toy and featured a doll's head on the top of a stick. It is, in actual fact, eighteenth-century in origin, but I've taken the liberty of introducing it here as a fitting accessory.

This is a really simple outfit to make. The fabric does not fray, which means that you do not need to hem it. If you use an alternative fabric, use Fray Stop along the hem or iron a lightweight bonding web or interlining fabric onto the wrong side of the fabric.

If you prefer hose to trousers, follow the instructions for the leggings pattern for the young squire (see page 95), enlarging the pattern to fit this portly character. I chose two different-coloured fabrics for the fool, but you could mix and match up to three or four colours for your the outfit.

Materials

1/12 scale male porcelain-bodied doll with portly physique

Two pieces of shiny fabric in contrasting colours

Two small bells or beads

Fray Stop glue

Tacky glue

Length of narrow braid

A small piece of wadding

Method

1 Cut out one jacket front from a piece of red fabric, reverse the pattern and cut out a second piece in gold (or substitute with your own colours). Next, cut out a jacket back in red, reverse the pattern and cut out a second piece in gold. Cut out one trouser section in red and one in gold. Cut out the hood in gold, reverse the pattern and cut out a second piece in either colour. Finally, cut out two 'horns' for the hood in pattern 'v'; these can both be in red, or one of each colour.

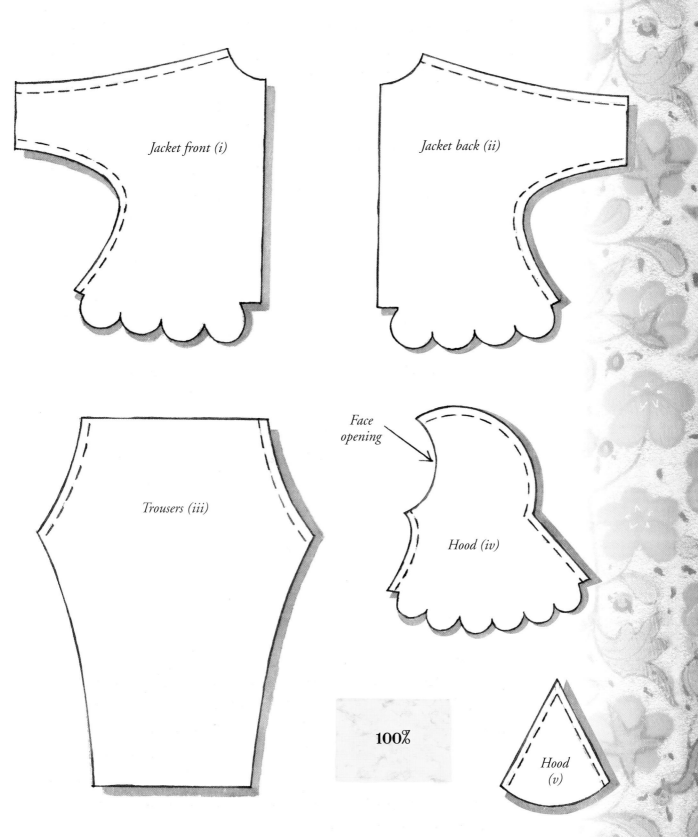

Jacket front (i)

Jacket back (ii)

Trousers (iii)

Face opening

Hood (iv)

100%

Hood (v)

2 With right sides together, sew the two back halves of the jacket down the centre back seam. With right sides together, sew the two fronts to the back of the jacket along the shoulder and side seams. Turn the jacket to the right side. Trim the sleeves at the wrist edge with a narrow braid and then check the fit against the doll. Use the same braid to fasten the jacket down the front and around the neck, carefully sticking the braid into place.

3 With the wrong sides of the trousers together, sew the front and back seams. Open them out so that the seams are at the centre front and centre back of the garment and then sew the leg seams. Turn the garment to the right side and fit onto the doll. You may wish to gather the fabric around the waist area. My fabric was slightly stretchy so this wasn't necessary. You can also trim the waist edge with narrow braid if you wish.

4 With the wrong sides of the hood together, sew the seam from the top of the head to the back of the hood, and from the front neck to the centre front, leaving the curved section open for the face. Turn to the right side, pull the hood over the head of the doll and down over the shoulders. Trim with narrow braid if desired.

5 Cut two pieces from pattern piece 'v'. Fold in half from the point to the curved edge and sew down the seams to form two cone shapes. Turn the shapes to the right side and lightly stuff with a small quantity of wadding. Stick the horns into place on the hood and sew small bells onto the points.

6 Finally, make a poupette for the doll. Cut a piece of very thin dowelling 2in (50mm) long or use a piece of cocktail stick. Sand lightly and stain, if required. Glue a small bead to one end of the stick and a tiny doll's head to the other. Gather pieces of lace, metallic fabric or other trimming around the head and neck of the poupette. I cut some of the shiny fabric into points and secured small gold beads at the ends to look like tiny bells. Alternatively, a marotte or poupette kit is available from some doll makers.

Medieval Knight

The knight of the eleventh and twelfth centuries was protected in battle by mail armour from many injuries. The mail was made up of interlinking iron rings. The metal fabric was shaped to fit the knight so that it was as comfortable and easy as possible to wear. Initially, it was worn to protect the upper body; only important knights or high-ranking lords wore any protection on their legs. This mail shirt or 'hauberk' was usually knee length, split at the front and back to enable the knight to sit astride a horse, and had elbow-length sleeves. Because chain mail could be pierced by arrows, a padded coat worn under the mail armour provided extra protection, absorbing the impact from the blows. It also helped to prevent the armour from piercing the knight's skin.

As time passed, plate armour replaced mail armour to protect more vulnerable parts of the body. In the late eleventh century and early twelfth century, the knight wore mufflers: mail mittens with leather palms. If he was wealthy enough, his legs would have been encased in mail chausses: a garment which covered the legs and feet, with leather soles. The neck was one of the most vulnerable parts of the body, yet in earlier armour, it was unprotected, exposing an area that could easily be targeted in battle. Later versions included a coif: a mail collar designed to afford greater protection to the throat. For further protection, a conical helmet protected the head, which had a nasal bar to help deflect blows from the face. By the twelfth century, it tended to be larger to protect more of the face, and the conical helmet more rounded to better deflect blows to the head.

Typically, mail armour weighed 30–40lb (13–18kg). Its main disadvantage, however, was not its weight, but the fact that it got very hot in sunlight. This was especially a problem in hotter climates, such as the conditions the knights

Three knights leaving a tournament from the Treatise on Devotion held in the collection of the Musée Condé, Chantilly, France.

encountered when taking up the call for crusades to the Holy Land. Heat stroke was a real probability, particularly because of the metal helmets. In order to deflect the sun's rays, a lightweight tunic or surcoat was worn over the mail hauberk.

The thirteenth century saw the addition of the helm. This was a metallic helmet with a flat top and a facial covering worn over a padded cap. Slits at eye-level and holes for ventilation at the nose and mouth gave added protection and comfort. The padded jackets were reinforced with toughened leather and the mail mittens developed into mail gloves with separate fingers. Plate armour was added to cover the knee area in the form of round metal plates called poleyns.

Hairstyles for men varied. In the early twelfth century, the hair was often worn quite long, even braided. Later, this became increasingly natural with long, wavy hair. Long, thin moustaches and beards divided into several points were fashionable in the early part of the century. From the reign of Richard I onwards (1189–99), the hair was worn shorter with a short curled fringe. Younger men tended to be clean-shaven.

Working in miniature

I have been asked many times if I would publish my knitting pattern for chain mail armour. I first showed the medieval knight at dolls' house exhibitions especially for miniaturists, but doll makers have also expressed a keen interest in him.

I have taken a few liberties with the chain mail. I tried to source a realistic fabric for it, but the results were disappointing; the mail did not look textured enough, the shape was difficult to achieve and the fabric was not sturdy enough.

I then tried to find a yarn that could be knitted to look like mail. Knitted fabrics can be moulded more effectively to the body of the doll, and give a better shape and mail-like texture. A metallic yarn was the obvious choice for mail, but finding the right one was not easy. Eventually, I came across a silver thread with a black thread twisted around it and this was just right.

There are some limitations in dressing medieval knight dolls at 1/12 scale. Too much bulk looks too heavy, so the first thing to go was the padded jacket, which improved the look of the mail. Instead, I used a small amount of wadding around the doll's limbs to replicate the jacket. The thread was quite difficult to knit, so rather than a two-piece suit of mail, I developed a one-piece with as little shape as possible. Once the coif, surcoat and sword were added, the effect was very realistic. While he is a fairly accurate representation of a knight from the 1180s, he is also an ideal Knight of the Round Table.

This pattern can be adjusted easily to fit your own doll. In my experience, it is impossible to produce a single pattern to fit all brands of 1/12 scale male doll as they tend to vary in shape and size. To help you with the pattern (see page 88), standard knitting abbreviations are applied.

This design can be altered in lots of ways to make your knight look very different. The front and back of the surcoat could be contrasting colours, or halve the pattern through the centre neckline to the hem and cut out each in a different colour, allowing a little extra fabric at the middle cut edge to rejoin the two halves. Stitch the contrasting colours back together and you have a two-coloured front and back.

Materials

1/12 scale porcelain doll, soft- or porcelain-bodied

Two pairs of size 19 knitting needles

Six packs of Madeira metallic yarn (5011)
for knitting and embroidery

Small pieces of black or brown leather
(for the mitten palms and soles)

Small quantity of iron-on double-sided fine interfacing
(for the surcoat)

Slubbed silk (for the two surcoat pieces)

Matching plain silk (for the surcoat lining)

20in (0.5m) very fine picot braid (to edge the surcoat)

Scrap of contrasting fabric
(for the motif on the front of the surcoat)

Black or brown leather for the belt,
approximately ⅛ x 8in (3 x 20.3cm)

Black sewing thread (to make up the outfit)

Sewing thread (for the surcoat, in matching colour)

Tapestry needle, size 24 or 26

Sewing needle

Fine-pointed embroidery scissors

Safety pin

Tacky glue

Glue syringe with a fine nozzle

Rotary cutter

Cutting mat

Steel ruler

Accessories (broadsword, scabbard, shield, helmet, lance)

Tips

- Be patient; it is slow work.

- Use a good light source, preferably daylight, but a good lamp fitted with a daylight bulb is almost as good, certainly to work with in the evening or in poor light.

- Use a magnification aid to help guide the stitches; otherwise, they can be very difficult to see properly.

- Count your stitches frequently as you work.

- Be careful not to split the metallic thread as you knit; it is composed of three strands that are very easy to divide.

- Take extra care when increasing or decreasing stitches.

- Do not try to knit too much in one session; knitting with metallic yarn can make your fingers sore.

- Before making up the pieces, including the surcoat, make sure you have all your materials and equipment ready in advance. It pays to be organized.

Method

1 Work the first half of the suit. This is knitted throughout in garter stitch (every row knit).

2 Knit the second half of the suit. Work the second piece in the same way as the first, then reverse the shape to mirror the first half by folding inside out before stitching the two halves of the suit together.

3 Next work the sleeves, creating two the same.

4 Knit the tunic skirt in one piece.

5 Assemble the pieces you have made. Wrap fine wadding lightly around the arms and legs of the doll. Secure the ends with a little glue. Using a black cotton thread, sew the back seam of the one-piece. Sew around the legs of the doll using ladder stitch so that the seam does not show on the outside.

6 Sew up the front seam of the outfit to fit your doll snugly. Sew the shoulder seams with ladder stitch. Sew the sleeve seams and then stitch them onto the body of the tunic on the doll. Stitching the outfit onto the doll in this way enables you to attain a closer fit.

7 Wrap the skirt around the waist of the doll so that the split is at the centre front of the outfit and slip stitch the skirt to the waist. Using ladder stitch, sew down the centre back seam, leaving a slit in the seam to match the front. The outfit now looks like a mail tunic with chausses. Pull the lower ankle edge over the feet and sew in place under the foot so that the feet fill the chausses. If desired, cut out a small leather patch for the sole of each foot, attaching each one carefully with fabric glue.

8 Knit the neck and head covering as one piece.

9 Assemble the neck and head piece. Sew up the seam at the top of the hood. Turn right side out. Place the hood onto the doll and ladder stitch the front seam of the neck protector. Run a gathering thread around the face edge of the hood and pull up slightly to gather the hood around the face of the doll. The hood may be worn pushed back off the face and head to the back of the doll's neck, or it may be worn up. The gathering helps the hood to stay in position around the neck. The mail collar or coif of the hood should lie over the surcoat.

10 Make the mail mittens. You will need four pieces, each one following the following pattern. These are worked without a thumb which, at this scale, would be almost impossible to achieve.

11 Assemble the mail mittens. First sew two pieces together, then turn right side out. Run a gathering thread around the wrist area. Fit the mitten over the hand of the doll. Pull up the gathering thread and stitch the mitten to the sleeves. Repeat for the second one. If desired, stick a patch of leather to the palm of each mitten.

12 Finish the knight's costume by making the surcoat. First iron a piece of double-sided interfacing onto the back of the slubbed silk and cut out two surcoat pieces from the pattern. Peel away the backing paper and lay the surcoat pieces right side down onto the

wrong side of the lining fabric. Iron again with a dry iron for a few seconds to bond the two pieces together. Cut the surcoat pattern from the remaining lining silk. You now have two surcoat pieces, each with a lining and a slubbed silk surface.

13 With the right sides of the surcoat together, and using matching thread, sew the shoulder seams of the surcoat. Open the piece out and lie it right side facing upwards on your worktable. Carefully glue a continuous piece of fine picot braid around the outer edge of the whole surcoat, starting and finishing at a shoulder seam. Glue another piece around the edge of the neck.

14 Cut out a simple shape from a piece of contrasting material that has been ironed onto another piece of double-sided interfacing. Peel away the backing and apply the motif to the front of the surcoat over the chest area of the doll. Iron again to attach the motif to the front of the surcoat. Alternatively, apply your own design to the front using the appropriate fabric/silk paints.

15 Slip the surcoat over the head of the doll and place the coif on the head and neck protector over the neckline of the surcoat.

16 Fasten the surcoat at the waist with a strip of leather wrapped twice around the doll. Hang the sword from the belt and secure at one side with a knot. The leather is best cut out using a steel rule and a rotary cutter to form a long, narrow piece.

17 Finally, if your knight is not already wigged, you can now do so.

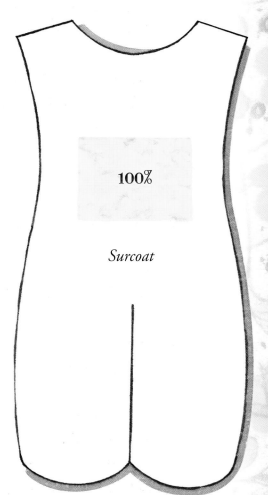

100%

Surcoat

Knitting pattern

Each half of the suit

Using No. 19 knitting needles, cast on 20 stitches.

Continue in garter stitch throughout (every row knit).

Knit until the work measures ¾ in (19mm) Increase 1 stitch at each end of the next row (22 stitches).

Continue knitting until the work measures 1½ in (38mm).

Increase 1 stitch at each end of the next row (24 stitches).

Continue knitting until work measures 2⅛ in (51mm).

Increase 1 stitch at each end of the next row (26 stitches).

Knit until the length of the leg is correct for your doll, measuring from the sole of the foot to the inside leg length.

Cast on 2 stitches at the beginning of each of the next 2 rows (30 stitches).

Knit 10 rows.

Next row: k4, (k2 tog) twice, knit to last 8 stitches, (k2 tog) twice, k4 (26 stitches).

Knit until the work measures from the sole to just below the underarm of the doll.

Divide for the armhole: k12 stitches, cast off 2 stitches, knit to end of row. Continue on the first set of 14 stitches (put the remaining stitches carefully onto a small safety pin) or, if you prefer, leave them on the needle unworked.

Knit until the work reaches the required length for the back of the doll's neck.

Neck shaping: cast off 4 stitches at neck edge.

Knit three rows. Cast off remaining stitches.

Rejoin the yarn to the remaining set of stitches.

Knit until the work measures to a length suitable for the front of the neck, approximately 4 rows less than the back of the neck.

Sleeves

Cast on 14 stitches. Continue in garter stitch (every row knit).

Increase 1 stitch at each end of next row and on every following sixth row until there are 30 stitches on the needle. Knit to the sleeve length required.

Cast off loosely.

Tunic shirt

Cast on 30 stitches.

Continue in garter stitch (every row knit).

Knit until work measures 1¼in (3.2cm).

Leave these stitches on the needle and with a spare set of needles, work another piece in exactly the same way.

Next row: knit across both sets of stitches (60 stitches in total).

Knit until work measures 1¾in (4.4cm).

Next row: k10, (k2tog), k10 (k2tog), k12, (k2tog) k10, (k2tog), k10 (56 stitches).

Knit 3 rows.

Next row: k9, (k2tog), k9, (k2tog), k12, (k2tog), k9, (k2tog), k9 (52 stitches).

Knit 3 rows.

Next row: k8, (k2tog), k8, (k2tog), k12, (k2tog), k8, (k2tog), k8 (48 stitches).

Knit 3 rows.

Next row: k7, (k2tog), k7, (k2tog), k12, (k2tog), k7 (k2tog), k7 (44 stitches).

Knit 1 row.

Cast off loosely.

Cast off 2 stitches at beginning of next row.

Knit 1 row.

Cast off 2 stitches at the beginning of the next row.

Knit 3 rows.

Cast off.

Neck and head covering

Using No. 19 knitting needles, cast on 47 stitches.

Knit 4 rows.

Row 5: k1, (k2tog, k7) 5 times, k1 (42 stitches).

Knit 1 row.

Row 7: k1, (k2tog, k6) 5 times, k1 (37 stitches).

Knit 1 row.

Row 9: k1, (k2tog, k5) 5 times, k1 (32 stitches).

Knit 1 row.

Row 11: k1 (k2tog, k4) 5 times, k1 (27 stitches).

Knit 1 row.

Row 13: k1 (knit 2 tog) across the row (14 stitches).

Knit 1 row.

Row 15. Shape the hood, (k1, increase 1 in next stitch) to end of row (21 stitches).

Knit 1 row.

Next row: k1, (increase in next stitch, k5) 3 times, increase in next stitch, k1 (25 stitches).

Knit 9 rows without shaping.

Next row: k11, increase 1 in next stitch, k1, increase 1 in the next stitch, k11 (27 stitches).

Knit 3 rows.

Next row: k9 (k2 tog) twice, k1, (k2tog) twice, k9 (23 stitches).

Knit 1 row.

Next row: increase 1 in first stitch, k2, (k2 tog) 4 times, k1 (k2tog) 4 times, k2, increase 1 in the last stitch (17 stitches).

Knit 1 row.

Next row: cast off 3 stitches, knit to the end of the row.

Next row: cast off 3 stitches, (k2 tog) twice, k3 together, (k2 tog) twice (5 stitches).

Cast off.

Chain mail mittens

Cast on 10 stitches.

Continue in garter stitch (every row knit).

Knit 18 rows.

Next row: (k2tog) across the row (5 stitches).

Next row: (k2 tog), k1, (k2 tog) (3 stitches).

Next row: s1, (k2 tog), pass the slipped stitch over the second stitch. Fasten off.

Young Squire

For the sons of nobility during this period, there was a heavy burden of responsibility. By the time he was six years old, the son of a nobleman would be sent away from home to be raised in another household. In today's terms, this might seem cruel, but it was considered vital in order to teach young boys the level of discipline required for manhood. The young boy would become a squire in his early teens and train for a knighthood. The training involved learning to hunt, how to ride and to fight as well as attend school with his peers to learn to read, write, speak foreign languages and the art of chivalry.

The young squire's role also included attending to the needs of a knight at jousting events. During a joust, if the knight was thrown off his horse, the squire was the only person allowed to help him mount his horse – no mean feat for a small boy considering the weight of a knight in full armour. The squire also assisted the knight with dressing, took care of his mail shirt, weapons and armour, and performed any number of other errands for him.

Working in miniature

You will need a 1/12 scale teenage boy doll for this pattern. In order for the close-fitting hose to fit properly, I recommend that you choose a doll with solid porcelain legs (see page 146 for suppliers).

Materials

1/12 scale teenage boy doll

Cotton mini-print fabric, 12 x 10in (30 x 25cm)

Jersey cotton, 12 x 10in (30 x 25cm)

Contrasting fine cotton, 6 x 5in (15 x 12.5cm) (for the hood)

Fine, black kid leather, 4in (10cm) square

Narrow, picot-edged braid

Sewing cotton and needle

Wide-eyed needle, e.g. a darning needle

Rotary cutter

Cutting board

Metal-edged ruler

Single small buckle

Small amount of wadding

Very fine black cord or thin strip of leather, 4in (10cm) long
(for the purse)

Tacky glue

Fray Stop glue

Glue syringe

Pair of fine scissors

Method

1 Using the templates provided, cut out one tunic back and one tunic front from the printed cotton. Reverse the tunic front pattern and cut out a second piece from the same fabric. Use Fray Stop along the edges of the cotton and leave to dry.

2 Cut out one hood section from the contrasting cotton, reverse the pattern and cut out a second piece from the same fabric. Use Fray Stop along the edges and leave to dry.

3 Cut out one section of hose from the knitted cotton jersey. Reverse the pattern and cut out a second piece from the same fabric.

4 Cut out two soles, two boot uppers and one purse shape from the fine kid leather. Make the leather soft and pliable by stretching it in every direction, working it with the fingers, before cutting out the patterns.

5 With the wrong sides together, sew the centre front and centre back seams of the hose along AB. Open out the hose on the wrong side so that the centre front and centre back seams are in the middle of the garment and then sew the legs of the hose.

6 Turn the hose to the right side and then place them onto the doll. Gather the top edge around the waist, with a running stitch if necessary. Trim the waist edge with matching picot braid.

7 With wrong sides together, sew the shoulder and side seams of the jacket fronts to the jacket back. Trim all the cut edges on the right side of the tunic with narrow picot braid except the front edges of the tunic. Fit the tunic to the doll, overlap the front slightly and stick or sew closed. Cover the centre front join with narrow picot braid.

8 With the right sides of the hood facing, sew along the stitching lines shown on the pattern. Turn the hood to the right side and trim all the raw edges with matching picot braid, including the area around the face opening. Fit the hood on the doll. The small tube shape at the back of the hood should hang down. Glue or sew the end of this to the back of the hood.

9 Using the rotary cutter, cutting mat and metal-edged ruler, cut out a small, thin strip of black leather as indicated on the belt template. Put the buckle onto the belt and put the leather belt around the boy's waist. Overlap with the buckle in front and stick down.

10 Use the sharp point of a pair of fine scissors to make small holes in the rim of the leather for the round purse as shown on the pattern. Thread a small amount of thin black cord or leather through the holes and draw up to form a small pouch. Put a tiny amount of

wadding into the pouch to give it shape. Pull drawstring up tightly. Attach the pouch to the leather belt at the doll's hip and cut off the surplus leather or cord.

11 Make the leather boots using a very small amount of supple leather. The boot upper does not need to be pre-shaped, as the shaping will be done as the leather moulds itself to the foot of the doll over the hose. Put some glue onto the back of the leather uppers and allow it to become tacky before applying the leather to the front of the lower leg of the doll. The upper border of the leather is the level that the top of the finished boot will be. Pull the leather to the back of the leg and foot, shaping it around the lower leg and foot as you go. Cut off any surplus leather so that the back seam meets but does not overlap. Make sure that there is enough glue along this seam to hold the shape together. Pull the rest of the leather down and around the foot, overlapping the leather onto the sole of the foot slightly. Cut off any surplus leather. Stick the sole over the bottom of the foot to conceal the leather overlap and trim to the shape of the foot. The boot is now complete. Make a second boot to match.

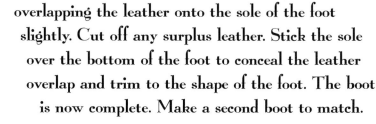

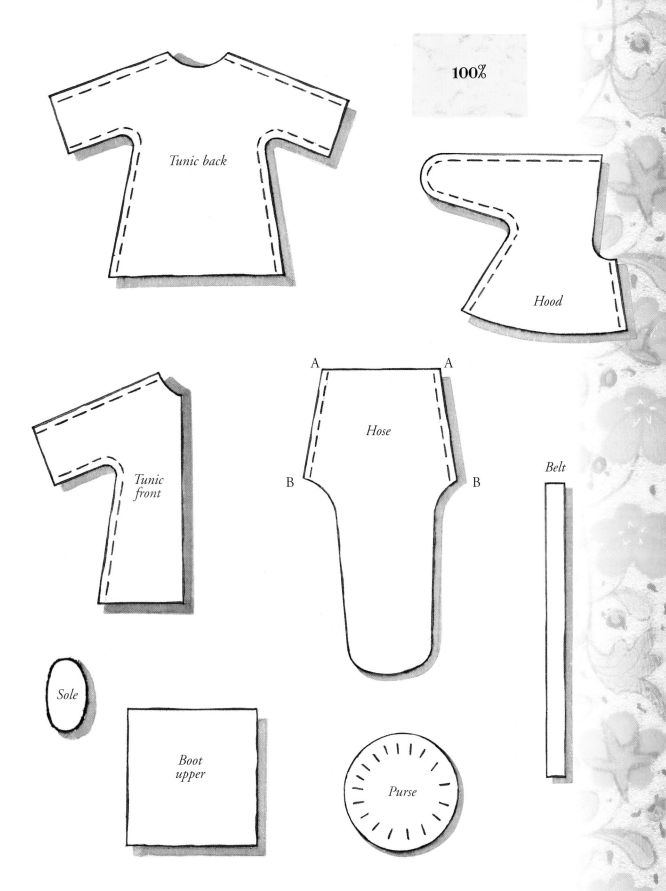

Tunic back

100%

Hood

Tunic
front

A   A

Hose

B   B

Belt

Sole

Boot
upper

Purse

Tudor Designs

Settle Cushions

Settles were the Tudor equivalent of a modern settee – but without the comfort! Often made of dark oak, they had a back rest and seated two or three people. As the years passed, they developed into more finely carved pieces of furniture, and some were used for storage. The storage seat was called the box settle.

Green diamond settle cushion

The design of the green diamond settle cushion is based on authentic Tudor motifs and colours, and is a relatively simple design to get you started. It was stitched in tent stitch and diagonal tent stitch (see pages 21–22 for stitching techniques) on 22-count canvas using two strands of stranded cotton. It is essential to use a frame of some kind (I used a tapestry frame) for this design to help minimize potential distortion in the canvas.

Materials

22-count canvas (or petit-point canvas),
9 x 6in (23 x 15cm), cream or white

Tapestry needle, size 24

Needle threader (optional)

Tapestry frame

Embroidery scissors

Magnifier (optional)

Stranded cotton threads,
1 skein of each

Stitch count

105 × 35

Design size

4¾ × 1⁹⁄₁₆in (12.1 × 4cm)

Alternative scales

Both cushions can be easily adapted
to other sizes of settle.

Method

1 Edge the canvas with masking tape and mount it to a tapestry frame.

2 Mark the centre point of the canvas.

3 Work the diamond pattern first, then the border and, finally, the background. Use tent and diagonal tent stitch with two strands of cotton in your needle.

4 To finish your piece, see page 34.

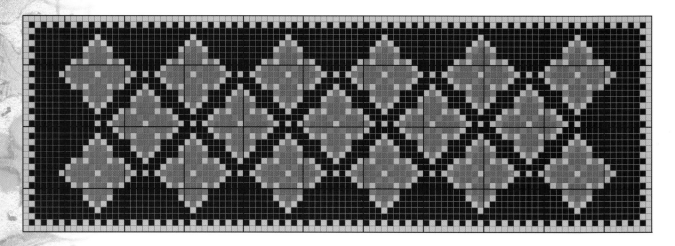

Thread key

	Colour	DMC	Anchor	Madeira
	Deep orange flame	606	335	0209
	Dark blue green	699	230	1303
	Leaf green	703	238	1307
	Light old gold	3820	306	2514

Thread key

	Colour	DMC	Anchor	Madeira
	Deep orange flame	606	335	0209
	Dark blue green	699	230	1303
	Leaf green	703	238	1307
	Light old gold	3820	306	2514

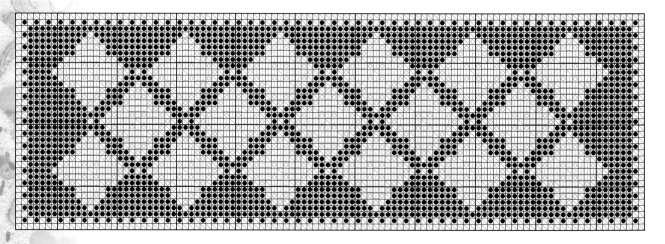

Acorn settle cushion

This second design is also stitched in a combination of tent stitch and diagonal tent stitch onto 22-count canvas, using two strands of stranded cotton. I've used an autumnal colour theme which seems appropriate for the period, but do feel free to experiment with alternative colourways. A change of background colour makes a dramatic difference to the overall appearance. It is essential to use a tapestry frame for this design to minimize distortion in the canvas.

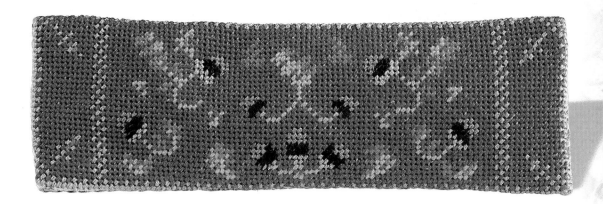

Materials

22-count canvas (or petit-point canvas),
9 x 6 in (23 x 15cm), cream or white

Tapestry needle, size 24

Needle threader (optional)

Tapestry frame

Embroidery scissors

Magnifier (optional)

Stranded cotton threads,
1 skein of each

Stitch count

105 × 35

Design size

4¾ × 1⁹⁄₁₆in (12.1 × 4cm)

Alternative scales

Both cushions can be easily adapted to other settle sizes.

Medieval and Tudor Needlecraft

Method

1 Edge the canvas with masking tape and mount it to the frame.

2 Work the border pattern first, then the acorns and, finally, the background.

3 For finishing techniques, refer to page 34.

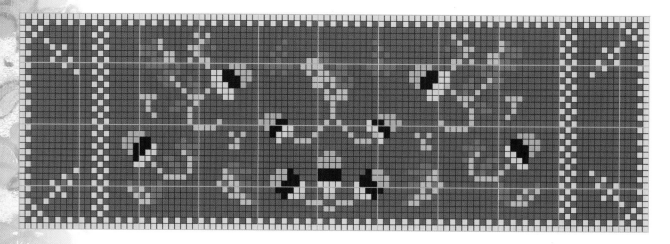

Thread key

	Colour	DMC	Anchor	Madeira
	Dark almond green	319	1044	1313
	Pale grey green	523	858	1512
	Flame	608	332	0206
	Light ash grey	648	900	1814
	Deep copper	921	1004	0311
	Golden orange	972	298	0107

Thread key

	Colour	DMC	Anchor	Madeira
	Dark almond green	319	1044	1313
	Pale grey green	523	858	1512
	Flame	608	332	0206
	Light ash grey	648	900	1814
	Deep copper	921	1004	0311
	Golden orange	972	298	0107

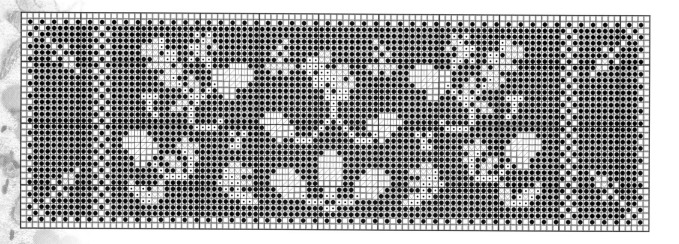

6atehouse Panel

This castle panel was inspired by the great gatehouse at Battle Abbey near Hastings in southeast England, which was founded by William the Conqueror in 1067.

Working in miniature

I have frequently been asked by miniaturists for wall hanging designs that include castles. This image is almost as popular as the dragon for designs of the medieval and Tudor periods. This panel is very easy to work while being remarkably effective. In fact, the smaller the design size, the more impressive it looks.

Materials

32-count fabric,
e.g. Murano (Lugana),
7 x 9in (17.3 x 23cm)

Tapestry frame

Masking tape

Tapestry needle, size 24 or 26

Needle threader (optional)

Magnifier (optional)

Embroidery scissors

Stranded cotton threads,
1 skein of each colour

Stitch count

64 × 144

Design size (excluding hanging tabs)

2 × 4 in (5.1 x 11.4cm)

Alternative scales

Count	Design size
14-count	$4\frac{1}{2} \times 10\frac{1}{4}$in (11.6 × 26.1cm)
24-count	$2\frac{5}{8} \times 6$in (6.8 × 15.2 cm)
48-count	$1\frac{1}{4} \times 3$in (3.4 × 7.6cm)
60-count	$1 \times 2\frac{3}{8}$in (2.7 × 6.1cm)

Method

1 First edge the canvas with masking tape and mount it to your tapestry frame.

2 Using your preferred method, find and mark the centre of your design onto the canvas.

3 Using tent stitch and two strands of stranded cotton thread, begin to stitch the design. The best starting point is the simple border pattern, to guide your stitching for the abbey in the centre of the design.

4 Work the outline of the central design next and then the clouds and grass. Switch to diagonal tent stitch to complete the background of the design.

5 For instructions on how to finish off your wall hanging, see pages 30–31. Like the Lovers in the Garden tapestry, the design would also look very attractive framed (see page 52).

The turrets of the gatehouse at Battle Abbey inspire this bold design.

Thread key

	Colour	DMC	Anchor	Madeira
	Light umber	436	363	2011
	Stone grey	642	392	1906
	Dark green grey	645	8581	1811
	Pale toffee	738	942	2013
	Dark sapphire	796	133	0913
	Baby blue	828	9159	1101
	Dark warm grey	844	1041	1810
	Deep delft blue	930	1035	1712
	Flesh	945	881	2313
	Deep sage green	3051	269	1508
	Grass green	3347	265	1408
	White	Blanc	2	White

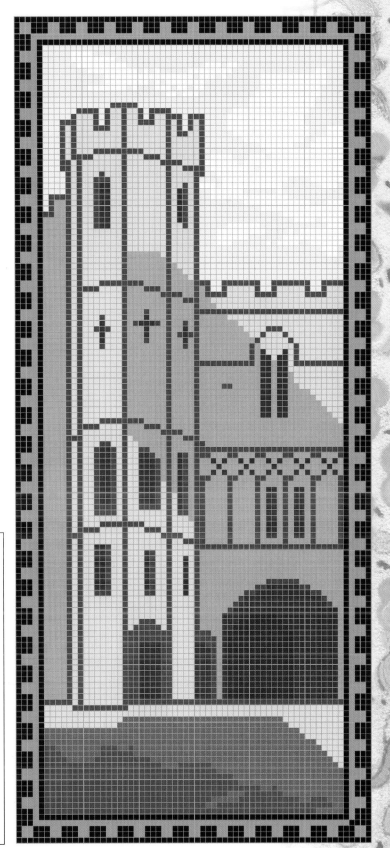

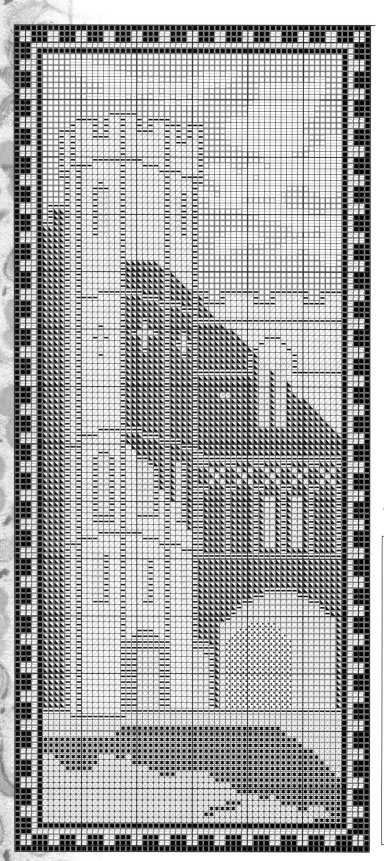

Thread key

	Colour	DMC	Anchor	Madeira
	Light umber	436	363	2011
	Stone grey	642	392	1906
	Dark green grey	645	8581	1811
	Pale toffee	738	942	2013
	Dark sapphire	796	133	0913
	Baby blue	828	9159	1101
	Dark warm grey	844	1041	1810
	Deep delft blue	930	1035	1712
	Flesh	945	881	2313
	Deep sage green	3051	269	1508
	Grass green	3347	265	1408
	White	Blanc	2	White

Peacock Table Carpet

Carpets were a luxury item in the medieval and Tudor periods. Their appearance in households of the day was precipitated by the return of crusaders from the Middle East who brought back with them the spoils of their travels, including decorative textiles. Too valuable to use as floor coverings, they were displayed on walls and tables as symbols of status. It was only in the most affluent households where guests could actually walk on these precious items. Carpets and wall hangings, linens and other soft furnishings were often passed on as heirlooms to subsequent generations.

Tudor motifs – like the peacock – feature in a well-known pattern book of the day: *A Schole-House for the Needle*, first published in 1632 by Richard Shorleyker. It was a compendium of lace-making designs, which could be adapted to other needlecraft techniques. Books of such designs were commonplace during this period. An original copy is exhibited in the lace department of London's Victoria and Albert Museum. It was out of print for many years but, in the 1940s, a complete copy turned up at a jumble sale, and the owners have since had it republished. As a result, the designs are once more available for present-day stitchers.

Materials

32-count evenweave fabric,
cream, 9 x 6 in (23 x 15cm)

Tapestry needle, size 24 or 26

Needle threader (optional)

Embroidery frame

Embroidery scissors

Magnifier (optional)

Stranded cotton thread thread,
1 skein of each colour (except
3047 which requires 2 skeins)

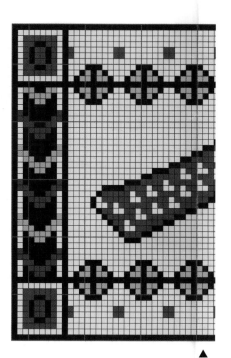

Stitch count

146 × 55

Design size

4½ × 1¾ in (11.6 × 4.4cm)

Alternative scales

Count	Design size
14-count	10½ × 4 in (26.5 × 10cm)
24-count	6 × 2¼ in (15.5 × 5.8cm)
48-count	3 × 1¼ in (7.7 × 2.9cm)
60-count	2¼ × 1in (6.2 × 2.3cm)

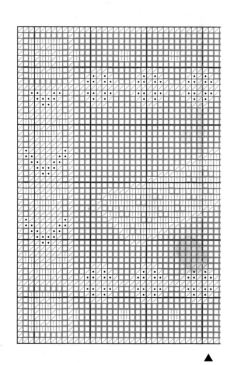

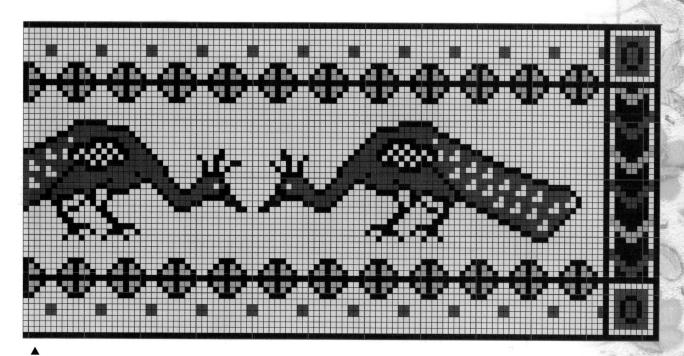

Thread key

	Colour	DMC	Anchor	Madeira
∷∷∷	Copper	922	1003	0310
TTTT	Darkest grey green	934	862	1506
▦▦▦	Straw	3047	852	2205
＼＼＼	Dark ocean blue	3808	1068	2507

Thread key

	Colour	DMC	Anchor	Madeira
	Copper	922	1003	0310
	Darkest grey green	934	862	1506
	Straw	3047	852	2205
	Dark ocean blue	3808	1068	2507

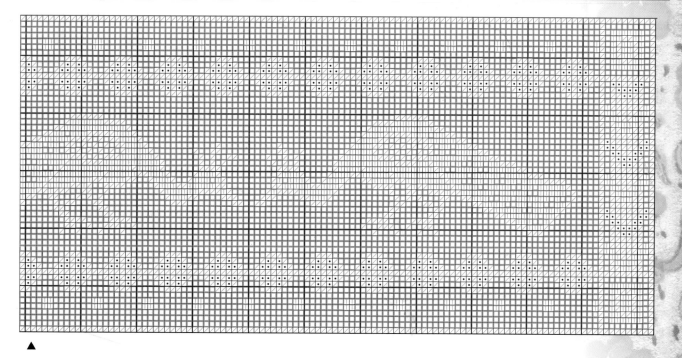

An example of lace making designs featured in A Schole-House for the Needle, *published in 1632 by Richard Shorleyker. Books of such designs were very popular in the Tudor period.*

Method

1 First edge the fabric with masking tape and mount it to a small tapestry frame.

2 Work the design in tent and diagonal tent stitch, using two strands of stranded thread in your needle. Begin stitching the round elements of the border for this design first; this will make thread counting much easier.

3 Next work the peacock design, followed by the outlines of the border and the small blue squares within the border design.

4 Lastly, fill in the border outline of the design and then the straw-coloured background.

5 For instructions on finishing your piece, see page 33. If you wish, you might add a fringed border or tasselled edging, attached to the short ends of the table carpet, which would make an attractive decorative addition to the piece.

Pomegranate Chair Cushion

This design is based on the 1480 borough arms of Chesterfield; the heraldic pomegranate design was a common one for the period. While the significance of the connection with the English town is uncertain, it continues to feature today; in recent times, the pomegranate has been adopted as the new name for the town's theatre.

Working in miniature

This design, while small, is quite difficult to reproduce with such a limited number of stitches. I have altered the shading a little so that the pomegranates stand out, while trying to remain true to the colours and design of the original arms. However, if you wish, the design can be worked using your own colour combinations. It is amazing how different this simple design looks in different shades of thread.

This design can be adapted to different chair sizes by stitching on a higher or lower count fabric or by altering the number of stitches in the plain parts of the pattern.

To fit the design to your chair, you can make a cardboard template of the chair seat. Cut out the template (see page 113) and use this to guide the number of stitches you sew around the template. Place the small template on your fabric and sew around the edge in your background thread. The sewing should extend beyond the template by at least a single stitch. Make sure that you have enough rows and stitches inside the outline of your template to complete the design in the central panel, then you can begin. Keep your cardboard template; you will need it to complete the seat cushion.

Materials

32-count fabric, e.g. Murano (Lugana),
cream, 5 x 4 in (12.7 x 10cm)

Small tapestry frame (tambour),
5 x 4 in (12.7 x 10cm)

Small embroidery scissors

Tapestry needle, size 26

Needle threader (optional)

Masking tape

Magnifier (optional)

Stranded cotton threads,
1 skein of each colour

Stitch count

62 × 49

Design size

Width at widest point: 2 in (5cm)

Width at narrowest point: 1½ in (3.8cm)

Depth: 1½ in (3.8cm)

*The 1480 borough arms of
Chesterfield is based on a
heraldic pomegranate design.
The connection persists today.*

Method

1 Edge the fabric with masking tape and mount it to your frame.

2 Work the pale green outline of the entire seat panel, then position the central design by working the outer ring and filling in the detail.

3 Work the pink background of the central panel and the rest of the pale green of the seat. Work the detail in tent stitch and the background stitches in diagonal tent stitch using two strands of thread throughout. If you use a pale-coloured 32-count evenweave fabric, you can omit the background stitching, and just work the central panel instead.

4 To finish, follow the instructions on page 32. If you prefer to adapt the design to make a wall hanging, adapt the design to fit a square background. It can also be adapted to make a dolls' house cushion cover.

100%

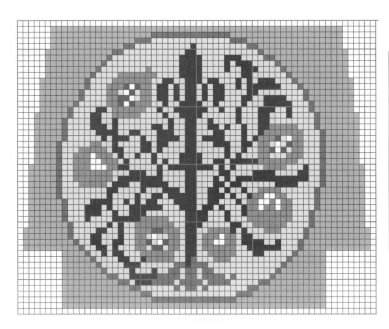

Thread key

	Colour	DMC	Anchor	Madeira
■	Deep grey mint	502	876	1703
■	Light oak brown	611	832	2107
■	Burnt caramel	780	309	2214
■	Green sand	832	945	2202
■	Flesh	945	881	2313
■	Pale mint green	3813	1042	1701
□	Natural white	3865	2	White

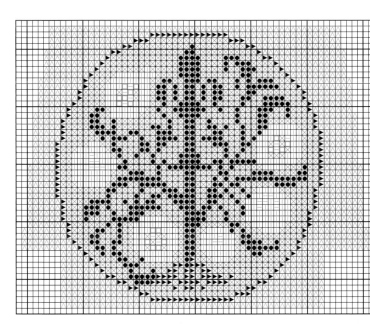

Thread key

	Colour	DMC	Anchor	Madeira
●●●●	Deep grey mint	502	876	1703
◄◄◄◄	Light oak brown	611	832	2107
▨▨▨▨	Burnt caramel	780	309	2214
‖‖‖‖	Green sand	832	945	2202
✕✕✕	Flesh	945	881	2313
ΛΛΛΛ	Pale mint green	3813	1042	1701
----	Natural white	3865	2	White

Tudor Bedspread

With the advent of a dedicated bedchamber during the Tudor period, elaborate beds, and luxurious bedding and soft furnishings became more common.

Originally called a posted, wainscot or sealed bed, the term 'four-poster' did not become commonplace until the nineteenth century. The bed was richly carved and the springs were made of cord which was laced back and forth across the bedstock rails to hold the mattress. More luxurious mattresses were made of wool or ticking sacks stuffed with feathers and down – swans' down was the best. Poor folk endured flock or straw, and sometimes gorse, leaves and seaweed.

The wealthy could afford the finest fabrics for their coverlets and bed hangings were made of silk damask. Sheets were fine-quality linen and blankets were made of kersey (woollen cloth) or fustian (cotton weft with linen warp). The less affluent had a coarser wool called fledge.

Richly embroidered quilts were imported from Spain and other luxury silks and cottons came from Italy, Syria, Egypt and India. Scarlet, a high-quality woollen cloth dyed red, was also used for bed hangings. For plain velvets and satins, embroidered panels, metal threads, spangles, braids and fringes were favoured methods for decoration, as was petit point or 'petepoynt'.

Working in miniature

This is a very pretty bedspread, inspired by authentic, popular design motifs of the Tudor period. The design is worked in needlepoint. I recommend that you use a cream or very light pale blue fabric if using the 32-count evenweave fabric so that you can omit the stitching for the background of the piece. However, if you prefer to stitch the entire panel, you will require an additional ten skeins of thread in this colour. I include a second colourway for you to stitch, if you wish (see pages 120–121 for the chart and thread key).

I used a miniature half-tester bed for this design, but the bedspread would look equally impressive on a four-poster. You can also use any of the individual panel designs to make hanging curtains and panels for the bed if required.

Materials

32-count evenweave fabric in ivory
(light blue or cream for the alternative colourway), 12in (30cm) square

Tapestry needle, size 24 or 26

Needle threader (optional)

Embroidery frame

Embroidery scissors

Magnifier (optional)

Stranded cotton threads, 1 skein of each
(except 739, for which 10 skeins are required for the background)

Alternative colourway:

Stranded cotton threads, 1 skein of each
(except 762 for which you will need 10 skeins for the background)

Stitch count

200 × 254

Design size

6¼ × 8in (15.9 × 20.2cm)

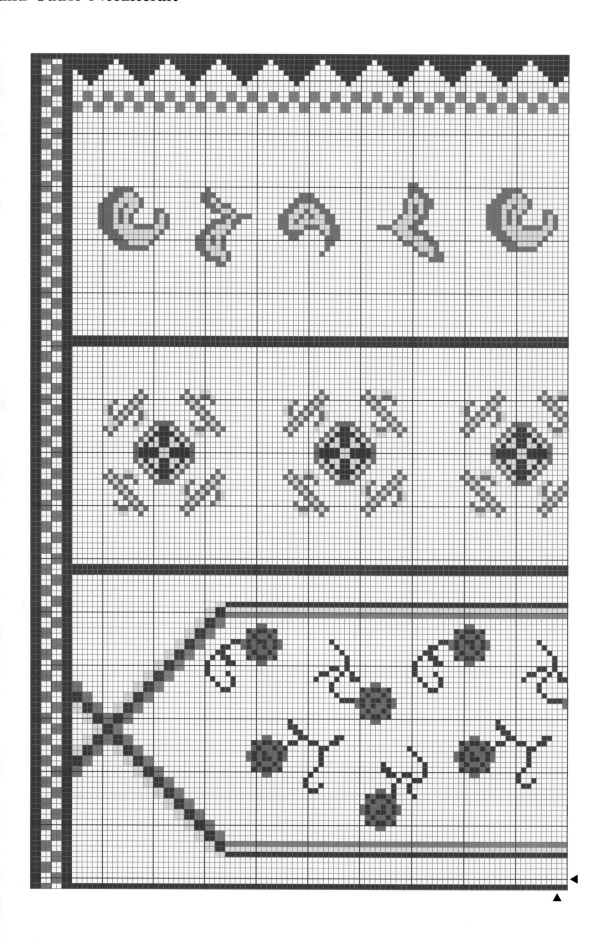

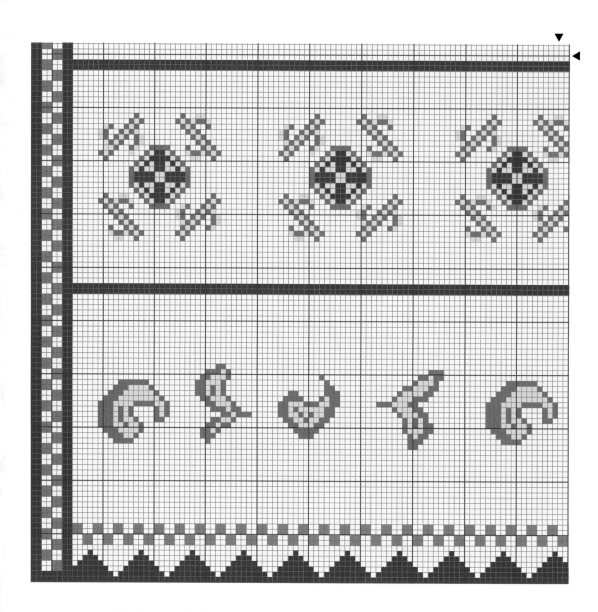

Thread key

	Colour	DMC	Anchor	Madeira
	Deep scarlet	349	1098	0212
	Dark leaf green	701	227	1305
	Dark primrose	725	305	0108
	Palest toffee	*739	885	2014
	Ginger	3776	1048	0308

Note

*only required if the background is to be sewn.

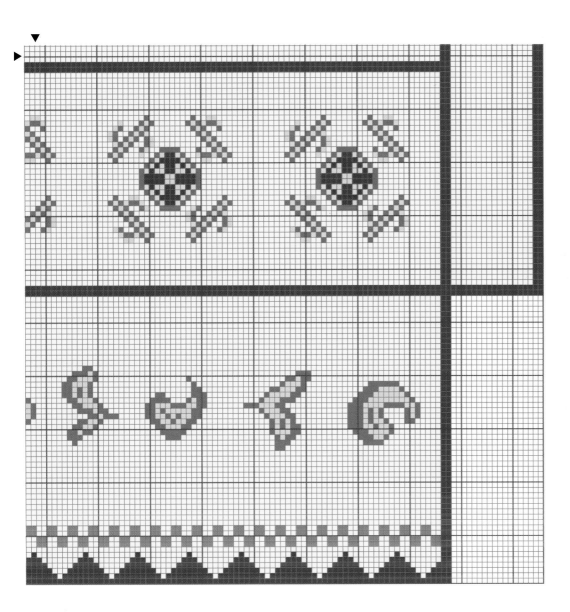

Method

1 First edge the fabric with masking tape to prevent fraying and then mount it to a tapestry frame. While, strictly speaking, you do not need a frame for this evenweave fabric, I prefer to use one to help count the threads accurately.

2 Stitch using two strands throughout and work the design in tent stitch and diagonal tent stitch. This panel is not difficult to sew, but be careful how you place the motifs and count your threads with caution. Stitch the outlines first, and then fill in the detail of each panel of the bedspread.

3 To finish, refer to the instructions on pages 32–33.

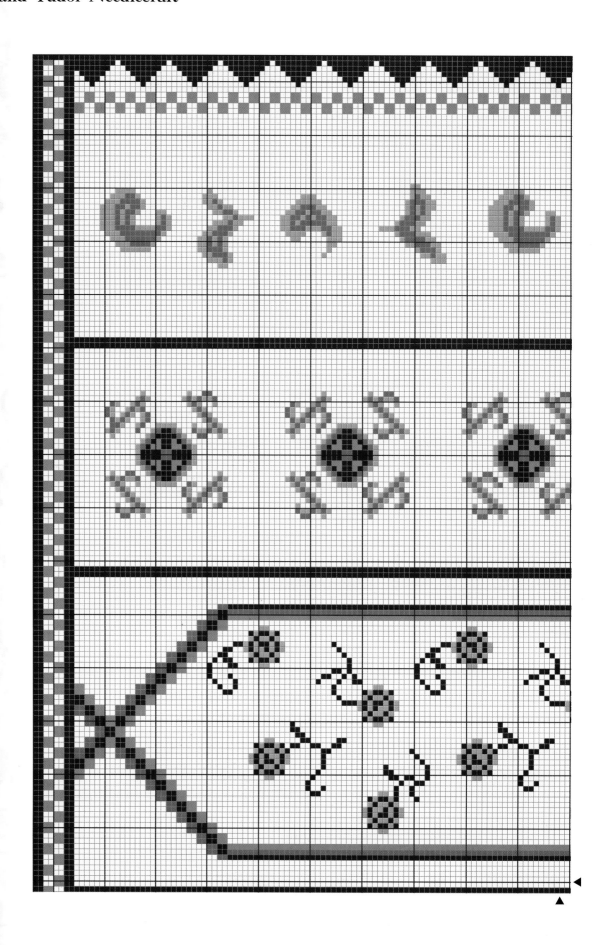

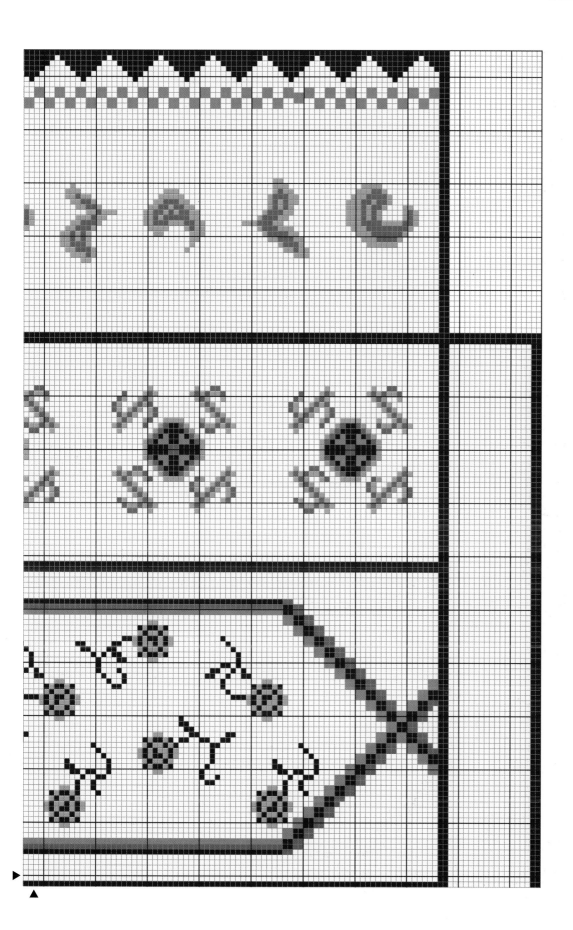

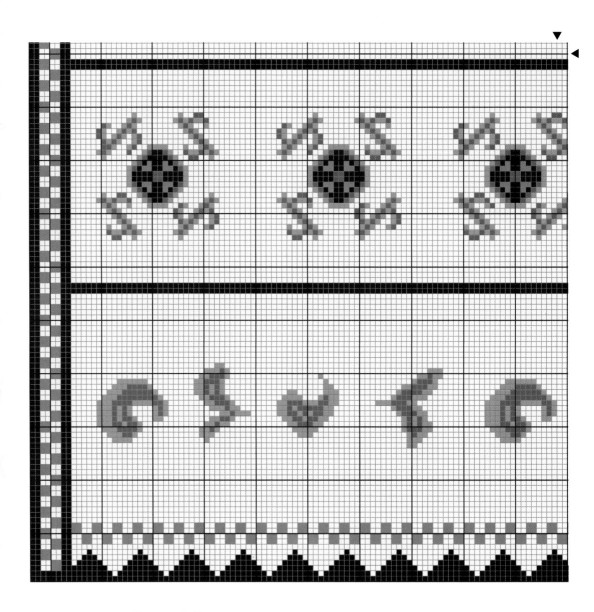

Thread key

	Colour	DMC	Anchor	Madeira
	Turquoise	807	168	1108
	Dark marine blue	824	142	1010
	Marine blue	826	977	1012
	Old gold	3852	306	1065
	Ecru	Ecru	387	2404

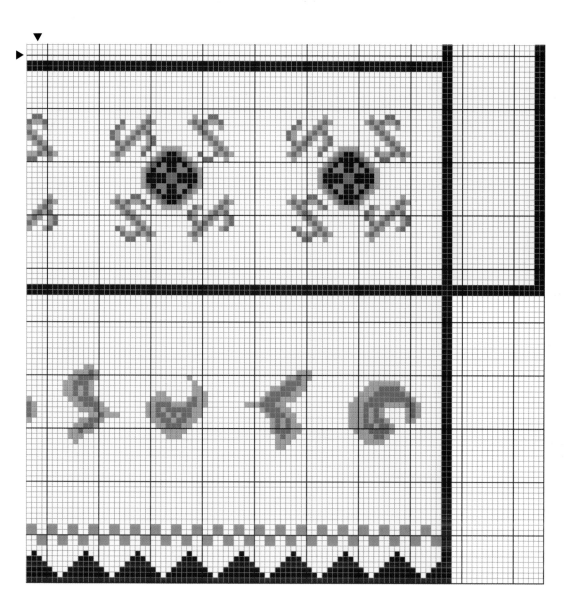

Method

1. As with the first colourway of the design, edge the fabric with masking tape to prevent fraying and mount it to a tapestry frame.
2. Stitch using two strands throughout and work the design in tent and diagonal tent stitch. Again, be careful how you place the motifs and count your threads with caution. Stitch the outlines first, and then fill in the detail of each panel of the bedspread.
3. To finish, refer to pages 32–33.

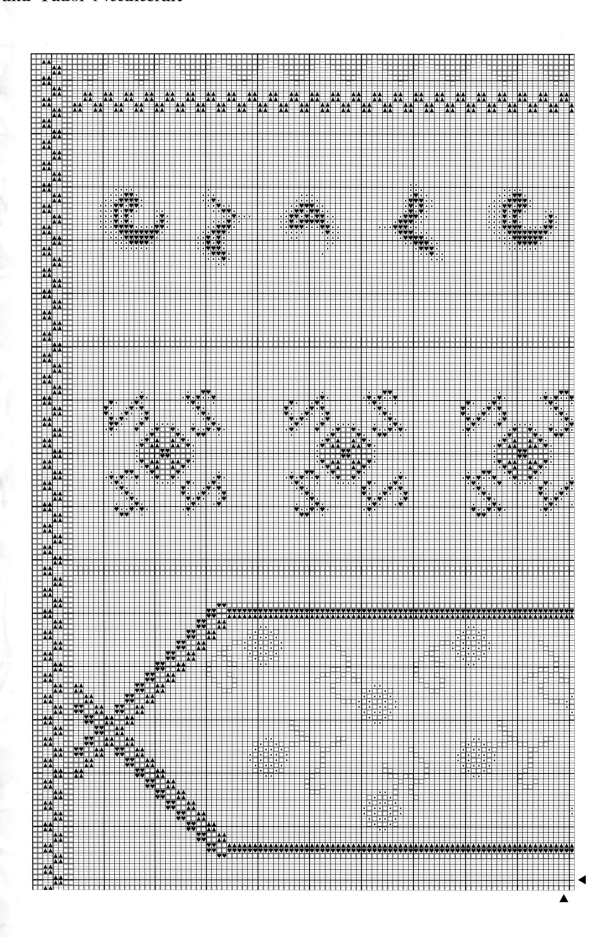

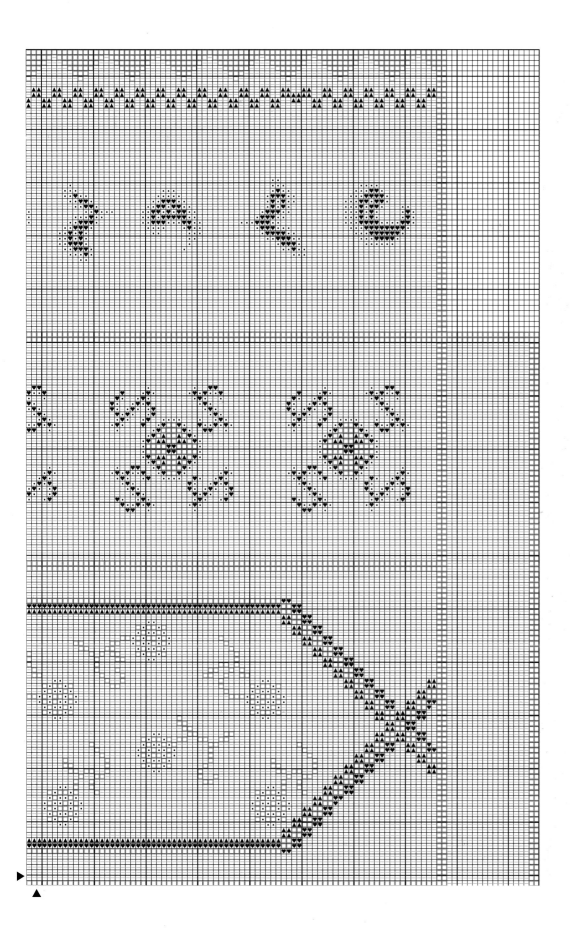

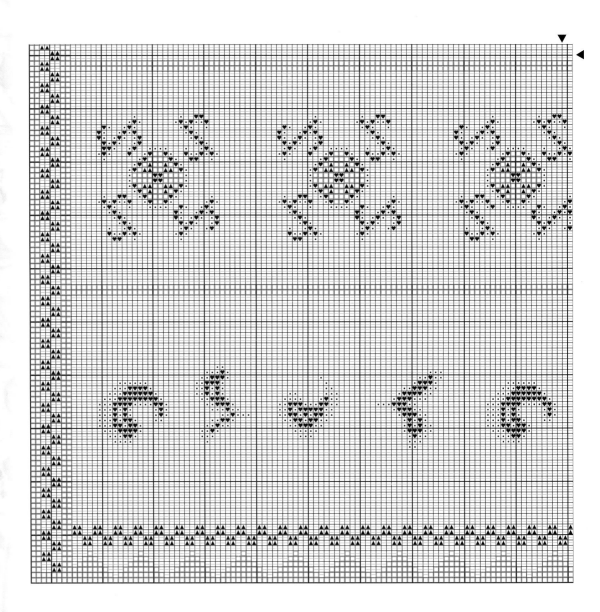

Thread key

	Colour	DMC	Anchor	Madeira
∷∷	Deep scarlet	349	1098	0212
▱▱▱	Dark leaf green	701	227	1305
♥♥♥	Dark primrose	725	305	0108
----	Palest toffee	*739	885	2014
▲▲▲▲	Ginger	3776	1048	0308

Note

*only required if the background is to be sewn.

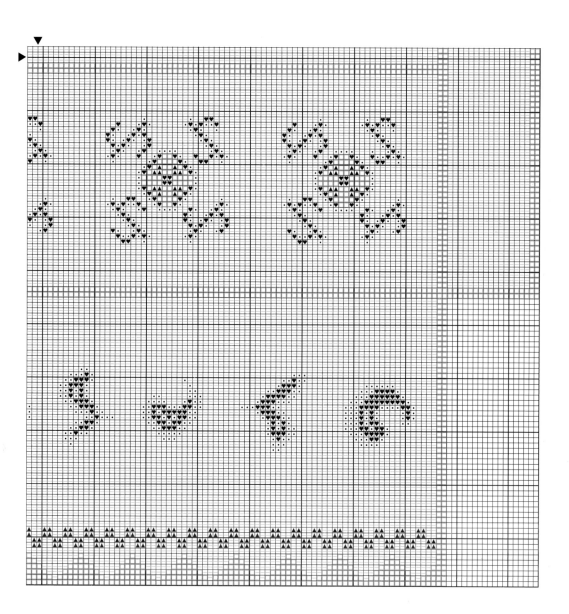

Thread key

	Colour	DMC	Anchor	Madeira
▲▲▲▲	Turquiose	807	168	1108
▢▢▢▢	Dark marine blue	824	142	1010
♥♥♥♥	Marine blue	826	977	1012
::::	Old gold	3852	306	1065
‒‒‒‒	Ecru	Ecru	387	2404

Tudor Noblewoman

Based on a sketch of the Countess of Lennox, this slightly masculine style would have been worn outdoors by noblewomen during the mid-1500s. This period favoured rich, dark colours in velvet, satin, damask, silk and leather. Heavy corsets flattened the bust and the waist was narrowed into a V shape. Padding was added to outfits in the form of hip rolls, sleeve padding and epaulettes. A full-length, lightweight chemise would have been worn under the garment and covered with a separate skirt and bodice. The underskirts had hoops to give shape to the outfit. The sleeves were fastened to the bodice with ties, and were either close-fitting and padded at the shoulder or full and richly embroidered with blackwork designs. Pannes or braids were used to decorate the sleeves – a very popular form of decoration during the reign of Elizabeth I (1558–1603). Linens and cotton lawns were worn underneath, and stiff, white ruffs added further elaboration.

Ladies' hair was worn away from the forehead and heightened with fake padding and coiled at the back into a caul. While the French hood was still popular, some women favoured hats similar to those worn by gentlemen. Accessories included rings, pendants, jewelled belts, gloves, feather fans, purses and lace handkerchiefs.

Working in miniature

The design converts well into miniature. Fine velvets, silks and brocades are suitable for the overdress, although they can be a little bulky at the waist. I used stretchy, non-fray gold fabric for the close-fitting sleeves and the lining combined with a burgundy velvet for the overdress and cream silk brocade for the inset panel. A gold mesh bag for chocolate coins was perfect for my noblewoman's hairnet and would make a great trim.

Materials

1/12 scale female doll with porcelain limbs

Blonde mohair (for the hair)

Silk or fine velvet, 12 x 10in (30 x 25.5cm)
(for the skirt and jacket)

Small quantity of silk brocade or silk

Lining fabric, 12 x 10in (30 x 25cm)

Piece of gold fabric or white cotton lawn, 12 x 10in
(30 x 25cm) (for the sleeves)

Fine cotton braid, burgundy, 4in (10cm)

Fine cotton braid with a double picot edge trim, white and gold
(to edge the jacket, armholes and sleeves)

Four small feathers and a fan-shaped jewellery finding

Pleater (medium)

Tacky glue

Glue syringe

Fray Stop glue

Sewing cotton in white and burgundy

Sewing needle

Medium pleater (with pusher)

Small amount of thin cardboard

Method

1 Cut out one skirt (i) panel from the fine burgundy velvet; one skirt
(ii) panel in silk brocade; and one skirt (i) and skirt (ii) panels in
lining fabric.

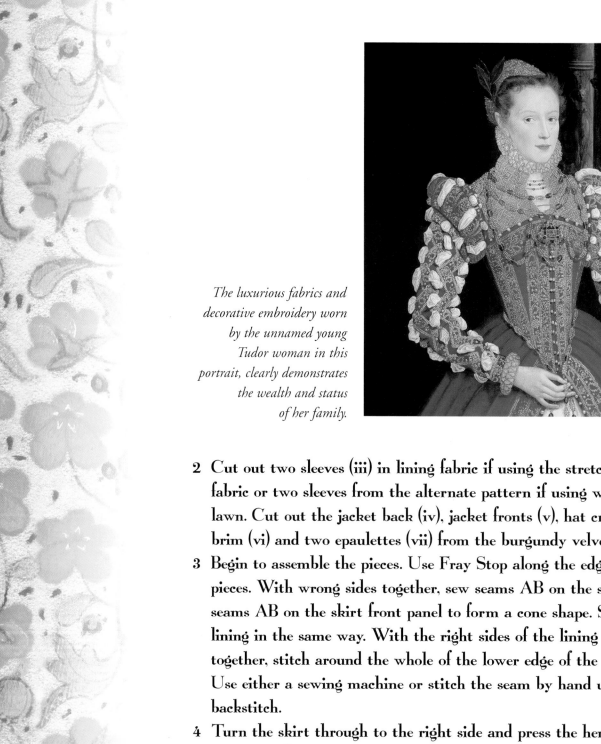

The luxurious fabrics and decorative embroidery worn by the unnamed young Tudor woman in this portrait, clearly demonstrates the wealth and status of her family.

2 Cut out two sleeves (iii) in lining fabric if using the stretchy, gold fabric or two sleeves from the alternate pattern if using white cotton lawn. Cut out the jacket back (iv), jacket fronts (v), hat crown and brim (vi) and two epaulettes (vii) from the burgundy velvet.

3 Begin to assemble the pieces. Use Fray Stop along the edges of the cut pieces. With wrong sides together, sew seams AB on the skirt to seams AB on the skirt front panel to form a cone shape. Sew the lining in the same way. With the right sides of the lining and skirt together, stitch around the whole of the lower edge of the skirt panels. Use either a sewing machine or stitch the seam by hand using backstitch.

4 Turn the skirt through to the right side and press the hem area. Do be careful when pressing velvet on the right side; iron with a cloth placed on top of the fabric to avoid marking the velvet. With the front panel facing upwards at the front of the garment, fold in along the pleat side on each side of the skirt panel (i) and press into place. Run a gathering thread around the waist edge. Position the skirt onto the doll and gather the waist up tightly. Fasten off securely.

5 With the wrong sides together, sew the shoulder and side seams of the jacket back (iv) and jacket front (v) pieces. Sew the sleeve seams and then insert the sleeves into the armholes and sew into place. Trim the edges of the jacket with the gold and white braid. Glue a prepared length of pleated white cotton lawn to the inside neck edge of the jacket. Dress the doll with the jacket and sew the front closed. If the fabric around the waist is too thick you will find that you cannot pull the jacket to a complete V shape at the front. If so, leave the lower edge of the jacket open; this will be trimmed with braid and look fine.

6 Next make the epaulettes (vii). These are intentionally quite large. Roll them into a long sausage shape, gluing into place as you go. Cover them with the mesh and stick into place. Glue the epaulettes onto the shoulders of the jacket along the armhole edge.

7 To decorate, add a chain of pearl-like jewellery findings in a gilt setting with glue along the front edges and across the back of the neck of the jacket.

8 If your doll is not already wigged, create a short hairstyle using some blonde mohair shaped in a pleater. Once covered, retain a small quantity of hair. Protect the outfit by wrapping the doll in cling film or placing all of it (except the head) in a plastic bag. Place the spare section of hair into a section of the gold mesh. Stick the mesh together on the inside and attach to the back of the head as though coiled into a caul.

9 Make up the hat by cutting out the pattern pieces (vi) from a piece of thin cardboard. Glue lining pieces to the inside of the hat if you would rather not leave the hat plain inside (although this will not be visible). Stick the ends of the brim together to form an oval shape that fits the circumference of the hat brim. Stand the oval upright and glue the hat crown to the top edge of the brim. Cover the whole hat in gold mesh to match the epaulettes. Take the mesh over the sides of the hat to the inside and glue it into position. Attach a small feather to the back of the hat, gently curling it forwards. Stick a length of narrow burgundy braid over the hat seam where the crown joins the brim.

10 For this project, I have used a pleater to make a small ruff for the neck of the jacket and the waves in the noblewoman's hair. To make the ruff for your doll, you will need a narrow section of cotton lawn, 6 x 1in (15 x 2.5cm). To make the pleated fabric for the ruff and the hair, see page 35 for instructions.

11 If you choose to use the cotton lawn sleeve, you will need to gather the upper part of the sleeve a little to insert it into the armholes of the jacket. This sleeve should fit more loosely and a little longer than the previous one. Trim the cuff with braid and then gather the cuff tightly around the wrist. If you wish, attach braid at the armhole and then criss-cross around the arm of the doll down to the cuff where you can fasten off or attach decorative braid, before inserting the sleeve to the jacket bodice. The first method allows the lawn sleeve to puff out naturally around the braid in a typical Elizabethan style. The braided sleeve has a panne decoration. The pannes are fixed only at the edges of the braid and otherwise left loose. The vertical strip of braid is glued along its entire length from the top to the bottom of the sleeve covering the central join of the side pannes.

12 To complete the look, paint the noblewoman's shoes in a matching enamel paint and add trimmings of small bows, gems or buckles. Paint the legs cream to simulate hose. Your doll can also wear a white cotton chemise underneath her outfit. If she does, leave off the sleeves to avoid making the outfit bulky.

Alternative hairstyle

For a different look, alter the hair and headdress. Make the hair long and swept back from the forehead over a tiny roll of padding to form a raised section at the hairline. Insert the rest of the hair inside the French hood at the back of the headdress. Use the template for the pattern for the French hood, and cut out from burgundy velvet. Cut out a second template in thick card and then glue the burgundy to the card.

Turn the pattern shape over and cut out a second piece from lining fabric. Glue this to the reverse of the headdress. Trim the edges of the headdress with braid and then attach small gemstones, rhinestones or other trimming to the edge of the headdress for decoration. Cut out the hood in fine silk to match the silk lining of the headdress. Use Fray Stop along the edges of the silk. With the wrong sides of the material together, sew the two edges of the rectangular back area together along AB to make a tube. Cover any raw edges of the tube section with a very fine matching picot braid. Place the back of the hair inside the tube of the hood and pull the shaped part of the hood up over the doll's head. Fasten this upper section to the hair once you have positioned the front of the headdress. The headdress should slope slightly backwards on the head and the two curved areas at the front should angle towards the doll's cheekbones. Position the hood section behind this headdress and glue into position on the doll's hair.

Alternative design

You might also like to try making this Tudor lady (below). Her dress is more formal and includes elaborate use of accessories.

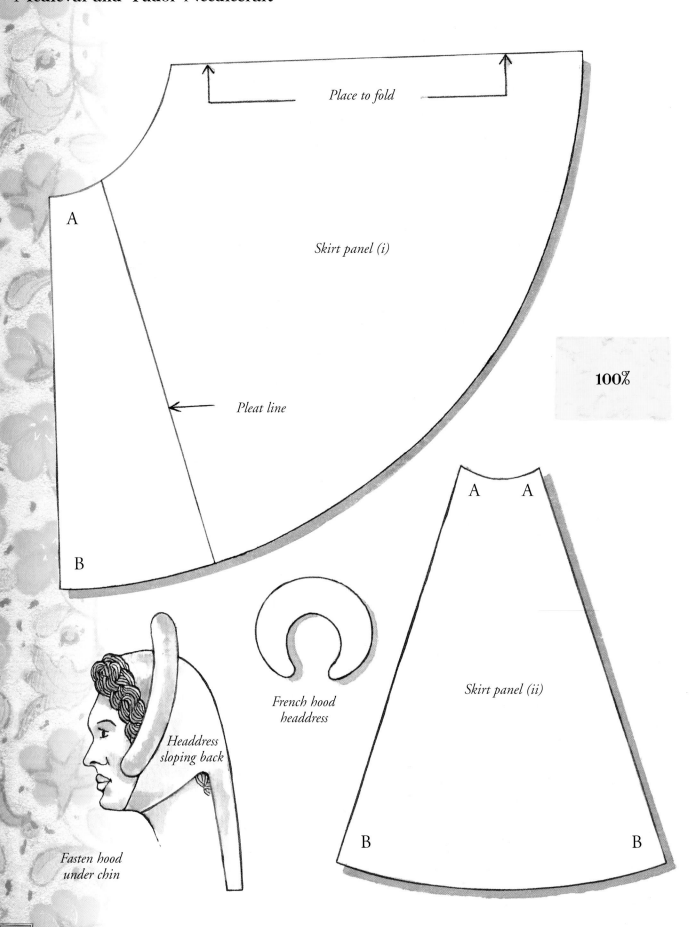

Place to fold

A

Skirt panel (i)

Pleat line

B

A   A

French hood
headdress

Headdress
sloping back

Skirt panel (ii)

100%

B   B

Fasten hood
under chin

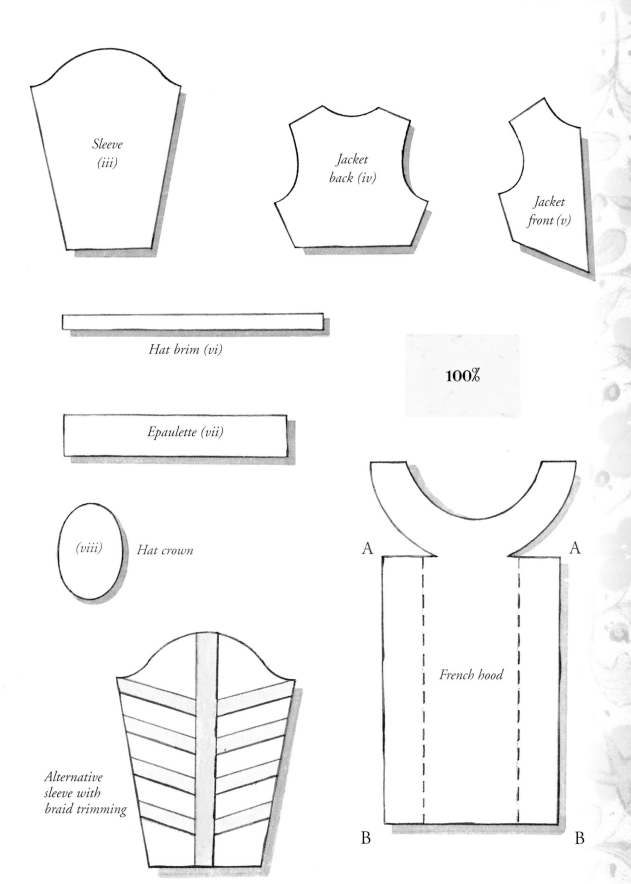

Sleeve
(iii)

Jacket
back (iv)

Jacket
front (v)

Hat brim (vi)

100%

Epaulette (vii)

(viii)   Hat crown

A   A

Alternative
sleeve with
braid trimming

French hood

B   B

Tudor Gentleman

By the latter half of the sixteenth century, fabrics were becoming brighter, despite the continuing popularity of black. The nobleman's dress consisted of highly decorative fabrics: silk, kid leather, cotton lawn, velvet and brocade. Braids and trimmings decorated the seams (so very useful for the miniaturist!), and embroidered plant and animal motifs were increasingly popular, as was blackwork.

Leather jerkins were fashionable, often pinked or slashed so that the undergarments were visible. Worn over a shirt, the gentleman's jerkin or doublet revealed frills or ruffs at the neck and wrists. The jerkin would have close-fitting sleeves and bodice with a short, stiff, flared skirt around the waist.

The undergarments consisted of close-fitting, cotton drawers with an opening at the front, tied at the waist with a drawstring, and a fine cotton lawn shirt with closely pleated frills at the wrist and neck. The opening at the front would have fastened with a drawstring or tied with ribbon.

Stockings or leggings were worn. Often, the fabric was too loose to fit properly and they had to be held up at the knees with tied lengths of fabric. Knitted stockings did not appear until the late 1590s.

The trunk hose would be composed of a foundation garment with pannes attached. Strips of braid were attached at the waist and leg openings, with the fabric underneath showing between the pannes. The stockings could be attached to the lower edge of the trunk hose, or tied to a nether hose garment or 'canions', which extended below the hose to the knee.

The outer garment of preference was the short, circular, lined cape rather than a jacket, which sometimes had false sleeves underneath which the gentleman would have worn a sword belt and carried a pair of gloves.

The younger gentleman usually wore his beard short and neat, accompanied by a moustache. The older gentleman had a fuller beard and his hair was normally neatly cropped. Hats were worn with a short brim and trimmed with small, softly gathered feathers at the crown.

Working in miniature

For this pattern I have omitted the gentleman's underwear as it only adds unnecessary bulk to the 1/12 scale costume, and it can't be seen once the doll is dressed. I prefer to use a doll with full porcelain legs as the hose look better fitted to solid legs. My doll wears a hairstyle slightly longer than might be considered authentic to the style of this period but, I confess, he was inspired by a favourite character of mine in a novel, and he is clean shaven for the same reason.

Young man against a rose tree (miniature), by Nicholas Hilliard (1547-1619), held in the collection of the Victoria & Albert Museum, London.

I have a sewing machine with an embroidery function that I have used to stitch a very simple decorative pattern onto the fabric used for the jerkin before cutting out the pattern pieces. If you like, you could also embroider the jerkin by hand with small patterns using a fine silk thread or, alternatively, use braid, which would be just as effective.

Materials

Slubbed gold silk, 12 x 10in (30 x 25 cm) (for jerkin and hat)

Fine black silk, 2 x 10in (30 x 25cm)
(for the foundation of the trunk hose)

Small quantity of black cotton jersey (or other stretchy fabric),
(for the stockings)

Fine picot braid, in coordinating colour

Length of narrow braid, black or alternative colour,
approximately ¼in (0.6cm) wide
(trunk hose trim at the waist and lower leg edges)

Small quantity of white cotton lawn (for the ruffs)

Small quantity of single-sided bonding fabric,
12 x 10in (30 x 25cm)

Soft kid leather, black (shoes and sword belt),
approximately 14in (35cm) long

Sewing threads and needle

Thin card

Tacky glue

Fray Stop glue

Glue syringe

Pleater (with pusher)

Rotary cutter and cutting board

Metal-edged ruler

Three small buckles (sword belt and shoes)

Single feather (to decorate hat)

Three or four black seed beads (to trim the hat)

1/12 scale sword

Method

1 Iron on a piece of bonding fabric to the wrong side of the jerkin fabric.
2 Cut out two sleeves, a doublet back, two doublet fronts (one a reverse
   pattern) and one collar from the slubbed silk. Use Fray Stop along
   the cut edges of the pieces, taking care to ensure the fabric is free of
   stains. (This may be less necessary if the pieces have a bonded
   interlining ironed onto the reverse.) From the remainder of the
   slubbed silk, cut out 11 tabs from the tab pattern (b) and two from
   the tab pattern (a), with one of these cut in reverse.
3 With the right sides of the fabric together, sew the shoulder and side
   seams of the doublet. Similarly, stitch the sleeve seams and insert the
   sleeves into the armholes. Sew them into place. Edge the tabs around
   the three shaped sides with narrow braid (I used picot braid). Stick
   the tabs from tab pattern (b) evenly around the inside lower edge of

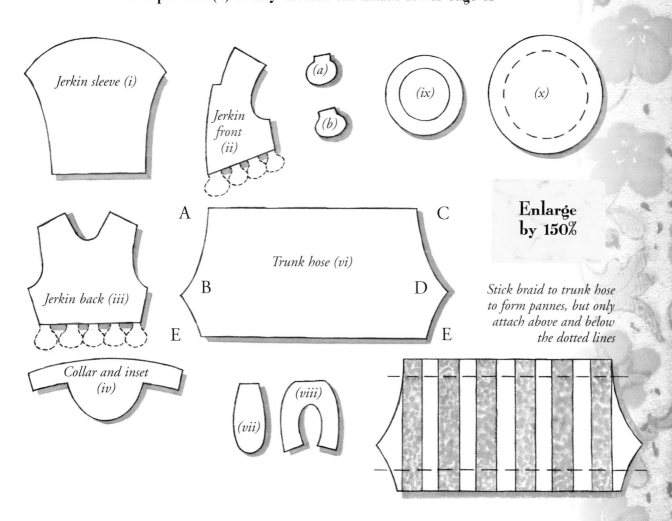

Jerkin sleeve (i)

Jerkin front (ii)

(a)

(b)

(ix)

(x)

A

C

**Enlarge
by 150%**

Trunk hose (vi)

B

D

Jerkin back (iii)

E

E

*Stick braid to trunk hose
to form pannes, but only
attach above and below
the dotted lines*

*Collar and inset
(iv)*

(vii)

(viii)

the jerkin. Leave a space for the other tab pieces (a) and stick these into place at the front lower edge of the jerkin fronts. Trim the doublet with pleated fabric for the ruffs at the neck and wrists (see page 35 for instructions). Add fine braid (again, I used picot) to the jerkin seams on the outside.

4 Draw around the side profile of the doll's leg from the toe to the upper thigh. Cut out the shape in paper or fine card to make a pattern. Fold the knitted jersey in half and position the hose pattern onto the jersey so that grain in the stretchy fabric runs from side to side. Cut out two stockings, one the reverse of the other. Sew along the back seam and then ease the stockings onto the leg of the doll. Glue the upper edge to the upper thigh of the doll and trim the upper edge of the stocking with a length of coordinating narrow braid.

5 Cut out two sections of trunk hose from fine black silk (one as a reverse pattern). Normally, these garments would have two sections: a close-fitting trunk hose and over this a baggier trunk hose to form a foundation for the pannes. I use only one of these for my doll – the baggier pattern – to eliminate bulk, particularly at the waist and gathered lower leg sections of the trunk hose. Use Fray Stop on the silk pieces.

6 Sew the trunk hose together, matching seams AB on each piece to form the front seam of the trunk hose, and then the seams CD on each piece to form the back seam. Open out the garment so that the front and back seams (currently at the sides of the trunk hose) are positioned in the centre front and back of the garment. Sew the seam on each leg from E on one leg to D and down to E on the other leg. Cut lengths of braid to fit the trunk hose pattern from waist to lower leg and glue only the top and bottom parts of the braid to the waist and lower leg of the right side of the trunk hose. Run gathering threads around the waist and lower legs of the trunk hose. Position the trunk hose onto the doll and pull the gathering threads tightly around its waist and thighs. Cover the gathered areas with the wider braid to form a waistband and leg cuffs, and glue these into position.

7 Dress the doll with the jacket, and stitch the front centre opening closed with tiny stitches.

8 Make the hat. Cut out one hat crown and two brim templates from the remainder of the bonded slubbed silk. Cut one hat brim pattern from thin card. Run a gathering thread around the outer edge of the hat crown. Glue one hat brim in slubbed silk to the hat brim card. Turn this so that the card pattern faces upwards. Gather the hat crown slightly so that the outer part of the crown can be glued into place on the hat brim. Stick the second hat brim shape over the hat brim section to cover the gathered section. Adjust the hat shape and trim the brim with narrow braid. At the join of the hat and crown, attach a feather. Trim with braid and decorate with seed beads or a jewellery finding. Glue the hat onto your wigged doll.

9 Cut two sole and two upper sections from the shoe pattern in kid leather. Stretch the leather in your hands before cutting the pattern out to make it pliable. Apply glue to the wrong side of the uppers and allow it to soak in for a minute before attaching the upper to the foot. Adjust the upper to mould the leather to the foot, maintaining a square toe shape. Gently pull the leather onto the sole. At the back of the foot, ease the shoe to a seam and trim off any excess. When the upper is in position, apply glue to the wrong side of the kid leather soles and apply these to the sole of the doll, covering the overlap of the uppers. If necessary, trim the leather to the shape of the foot. Slashed leather was in fashion at this time, so I snipped V-shaped nicks in the leather uppers before applying them to the doll's feet.

10 For the belt, cut a narrow length of leather with a rotary cutter and metal-edged ruler. For a thin, even cut, make one long cut to get a straight edge, then move the metal-edged ruler slightly to form a narrow belt and cut a parallel length of leather. The belt should be about 14in (35cm) long and less than ¼in (6mm) wide. Wrap the belt once around the doll's waist and tie in a knot at one side. At the other side of the doll's body, use the remaining length of leather to dangle the sword from the waist.

Appendix

Questions and Answers

Can the tapestry charts be used for cross stitch designs?

Yes, you can use cross stitches instead of the tapestry stitches but you may find that if you are working on 22- or 32-count fabric that you need only one strand of thread in your needle instead of two.

How can I alter the designs to fit my own dolls' house furniture?

These designs have been made to fit 1/12 scale dolls' house furniture and rooms. To adjust the size or form of a design, first make a paper template of the item you want to cover, for example a settle seat, chair seat, stool, bed, etc. Place the template on the top of your chosen evenweave fabric and stitch a single line of tent stitch in a different colour to the other stitches you will make around the outside of the template. Remove the template and count the number of threads both across and down inside the template area. Check the pattern for the design's stitch count.

If you have more threads on your design area than stitches on the pattern, simply work the extra threads into the border design. If you have less, then make sure that reducing the number of rows and stitches will not significantly affect the design. Try to reduce stitches where there is little or no pattern, or take a repeat or two out of a border design.

Why does canvas distort more than evenweave fabric?

Canvas has a stiffening agent on it that keeps the fabric taut and the threads in line. As the material is handled, this softens the canvas and makes it more pliable but it can also mean that the threads pull out of shape as you stitch. Some areas of the canvas may become more distorted than others. By fastening the canvas tightly to a frame, the canvas has a better chance of staying in shape. Evenweave fabric does not suffer from distortion as the threads do not have a stiffening component and are more densely woven.

Is it best to use a tapestry or embroidery frame for the designs?

Embroidery hoops (ring or tambour frames) can be used for evenweave fabrics, but for miniature work I prefer to be able to see the whole design on a tapestry frame. It also helps to keep the fabric taut and I can count the threads for the designs easily. The same is true for canvases. Mounting the canvas to a tambour frame also means more handling which can distort the fabric.

Can I alter the scale of the designs for different-sized dolls' houses?

Some designs include conversions for other scales. To work out the size of your finished project, divide the number of stitches for the design by your fabric count and this will give you a project size in inches. Once you have your desired scale, follow the instructions for making the pattern fit, as above.

Why are imperial measurements used for dolls' house scales?

Traditionally, craft measurements are given in imperial rather than metric. Wood, for example, is still cut in fractions of an inch, and dolls' house scales are normally referred to in inches, too: 1/16, 1/12, 1/24, etc. Thread counts are calculated by the number of threads per inch (or *tpi*). It is confusing to convert from metric to imperial unless the whole system is geared up, too, but to overcome the problem, I provide the metric conversions in brackets, and a conversion table is provided on page 148.

What is the best way to assemble and fit costumes to a miniature doll?

Sometimes it is quite difficult to assemble the whole of a 1/12 scale outfit before fitting it to your chosen doll, often because of the period style of the garment. Some costumes need to be assembled up to the point at which you stitch or glue the seams in place, and the garment is fitted at that stage. Once partially costumed, you can finish assembling the remaining seams until the doll is fully dressed. Once fitted to the doll and secured with glue or stitching, of course, the garment can't be removed, which is fine with a doll intended to be a collector's item, but less so for a toy.

Can the designs be adapted?

The designs can be easily adapted to other items. The designs for the wall hangings have been adapted for use as framed pictures, greetings cards, cushion panels, dolls' house carpets and bedhead hangings. I'm sure that you can think of many other uses, too. Circular designs such as the pomegranate design in this book can be easily adapted to greetings cards, but also look great as coasters or trinket box lids if you stitch them on a fabric with fewer stitches to the inch in order to enlarge the design. On fine fabrics with a higher count and silk gauzes, some designs can be adapted to make a lovely brooch or pendant. You can adapt any charted design; the only limit is your own imagination. Just use the stitch count of the pattern and the thread count of your fabric to determine the finished pattern sizes.

Suppliers and Sources of Information

This guide lists mail order suppliers for some of the materials and accessories used for designs in this book, related items for the dolls' house and useful sources.

United Kingdom

Tudor Times Miniatures
Silverweed Cottage
East Coker
Yeovil
Somerset BA22 9JY
Tel: 01935 863821
Website:
www.dollshousehomepage.co.uk
1/12 scale Tudor and Jacobean oak furniture. I used their half tester bed, court buffet table and an armchair in this book.

Willow Fabrics
95 Town Lane
Mobberley
Knutsford
Cheshire WA16 7HH
Tel: 01565 872225
Website: www.willowfabrics.com
Embroidery fabrics and threads by Anchor, Madeira, Kreinik and Caron.

The Dolls' House Draper
PO Box 128
Lightcliffe
Halifax
West Yorkshire HX3 8RN
Tel: 01422 201275
Fabrics suitable for dolls' houses, glue and glue syringes, braid, leather and other haberdashery items.

The Silk Route
Cross Cottage
Cross Lane
Frimley Green
Surrey GU16 6LN
Tel: 01252 835781
Supplies silk fabrics and threads.

Katy Sue Dolls
Unit 201 Tedco
Henry Robinson Way
South Shields NE33 1RF
Tel: 0191 4274571
1/12 scale porcelain dolls.

Fantasy Fabrics
Greenmantle
Plough Lane
Christleton
Chester CH3 7BA
Tel: 01244 335296
Great selection of fabrics for the dolls' house.

Annie Willis
Fine Design
21 Shawley Crescent
Epsom Downs
Surrey KT185PQ
Tel: 01737 210886
Tudor food, accessories, footwear and artefacts.

Sue Harrington Dolls
51 Old Fort Road
Shoreham-by-Sea
West Sussex BN43 5 RL
Tel: 01273 464670
1/12 scale porcelain dolls.

Sandra Whitehead

Knight Time Miniatures

8 Durham Avenue

Grassmoor

Chesterfield

Derbyshire S42 5DL

Tel: 01246 852467

Website:

www.knighttimeminiatures.co.uk

Frames, magnifiers, Celtic,
medieval and Tudor needlepoint
kits, miniature print fabrics
suitable for medieval and Tudor
1/12 scale, Congress cloth,
22-count canvas and 32-count
evenweave fabrics in small
quantities, hanging rods and
other accessories.

Tony Knott

Chapel House

Chipping Norton

Oxfordshire OX7 5SZ

Tel: 01608 641861

Antique-style pewter, armour,
weapons, castles, medieval and
Tudor commissions.

Les Chats

26 George Street

Ryhill

Wakefield

West Yorkshire WF4 2DE

Tel: 01226 725829

1/12 scale horses.

The Dixie Collection

4 Coneyhall Parade

Kingway

Coney Hall

West Wickham

Kent BR4 9JB

Tel: 020 8462 0700

Website: www.dixiecollection.com

Supplier of accessories for the dolls'
house including haberdashery items.

Sue Cook

Unit 5

Arundel Mews

Arundel Place

Brighton

East Sussex BN2 1GD

Tel: 01273 603054

Website:

www.suecookminiatures.com

Architectural plaster mouldings for
Dolls' houses and models.

The Polymer Clay Pit

Meadow Rise

Wortham

Diss

Norfolk IP22 1SQ

Tel: 01379–646019

Fax: 01379–646016

Website:

www.heaser.demon.co.uk

Useful resource for Fimo products
to make your own character figures.

The Dolls House

Market Place

Northleach

Cheltenham GL54 3EJ

Tel: 01451 860431

England's first specialist shop, with
a vast range of miniature
accessories and products.

North America

Nancy's Dollhouses
& Miniatures

1269 Airport-Pulling Road

South

Naples

Florida 34104

Tel: (941) 659 1444

Website:

www.nancysdollhouses.com

Dolls' house shop specializing in
the finest artisans.

Books

Carrington, James

1/12 Scale Character Figures
for the Dolls' House

Guild of Master Craftsman

Publications Ltd, Lewes,

East Sussex, UK

ISBN: 1 86108 161 8

Inspiring guide to making your
own period character figures.

Metric Conversion Table

inches to millimetres

inches	mm	inches	mm	inches	mm
1/8	3	9	229	30	762
1/4	6	10	254	31	787
3/8	10	11	279	32	813
1/2	13	12	305	33	838
5/8	16	13	330	34	864
3/4	19	14	356	35	889
7/8	22	15	381	36	914
1	25	16	406	37	940
1 1/4	32	17	432	38	965
1 1/2	38	18	457	39	991
1 3/4	44	19	483	40	1016
2	51	20	508	41	1041
2 1/2	64	21	533	42	1067
3	76	22	559	43	1092
3 1/2	89	23	584	44	1118
4	102	24	610	45	1143
4 1/2	114	25	635	46	1168
5	127	26	660	47	1194
6	152	27	686	48	1219
7	178	28	711	49	1245
8	203	29	737	50	1270

About the Author

Sandra Whitehead lives with her family in Grassmoor, a small mining village in Derbyshire, England.

Early retirement from lecturing at senior level on diagnostic radiography enabled Sandra to pursue her lifelong interest in books. She has a veritable library, ranging in subject from history, art, dolls' house and miniatures, historical costume, textiles and needlework. She is also passionate about photography, researching her family history, and visiting National Trust properties.

Almost every one of Sandra's interests, in one way or another, combine to inform her work in period miniature embroidery. In 1998, she set up what is now a successful small company, Knight Time Miniatures, which produces designs for period wall hangings for the dolls' house market. In 1999, encouraged by the response to this venture, she was inspired to write her first book *Celtic, Medieval and Tudor Wall Hangings in 1/12 Scale Needlepoint*, also published by GMC Publications.

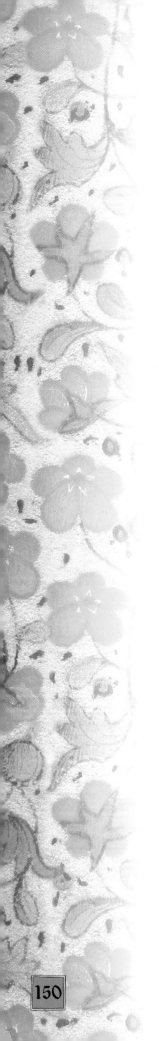

Acknowledgements

Through the publication of my first book *Celtic, Medieval and Tudor Wallhangings in 1/12 Scale Needlepoint*, I have made a great many friends. Their enthusiasm for my work and encouragement have led me to widen the scope of miniature needlecraft in this, my second book.

I am indebted to everyone involved in the making of this book: Kylie Johnston for her editorial help and support, Tim Mayer for the book and cover design, Anthony Bailey for the photography and John Yates, the illustrator, who has somehow managed to turn my pathetic sketches into comprehensive diagrams. Lastly, I'd like to thank my husband, Rob, for his help with some of the computer work and to my family for suffering an acute lack of attention during the last year.

Index

TITLES AVAILABLE FROM
GMC Publications
BOOKS

UPHOLSTERY

The Upholsterer's Pocket Reference Book	*David James*
Upholstery: A Complete Course (Revised Edition)	*David James*
Upholstery Restoration	*David James*
Upholstery Techniques & Projects	*David James*
Upholstery Tips and Hints	*David James*

TOYMAKING

Scrollsaw Toy Projects	*Ivor Carlyle*
Scrollsaw Toys for All Ages	*Ivor Carlyle*

DOLLS' HOUSE AND MINIATURES

1/12 Scale Character Figures for the Dolls' House	*James Carrington*
Americana in 1/12 Scale: 50 Authentic Projects	
	Joanne Ogreenc & Mary Lou Santovec
Architecture for Dolls' Houses	*Joyce Percival*
The Authentic Georgian Dolls' House	*Brian Long*
A Beginners' Guide to the Dolls' House Hobby	*Jean Nisbett*
Celtic, Medieval and Tudor Wall Hangings in 1/12 Scale Needlepoint	
	Sandra Whitehead
Creating Decorative Fabrics: Projects in 1/12 Scale	*Janet Storey*
The Dolls' House 1/24 Scale: A Complete Introduction	*Jean Nisbett*
Dolls' House Accessories, Fixtures and Fittings	*Andrea Barham*
Dolls' House Furniture: Easy-to-Make Projects in 1/12 Scale	*Freida Gray*
Dolls' House Makeovers	*Jean Nisbett*
Dolls' House Window Treatments	*Eve Harwood*
Easy to Make Dolls' House Accessories	*Andrea Barham*
Edwardian-Style Hand-Knitted Fashion for 1/12 Scale Dolls	
	Yvonne Wakefield
How to Make Your Dolls' House Special: Fresh Ideas for Decorating	
	Beryl Armstrong
Make Your Own Dolls' House Furniture	*Maurice Harper*
Making Dolls' House Furniture	*Patricia King*
Making Georgian Dolls' Houses	*Derek Rowbottom*
Making Miniature Chinese Rugs and Carpets	*Carol Phillipson*
Making Miniature Food and Market Stalls	*Angie Scarr*
Making Miniature Gardens	*Freida Gray*
Making Miniature Oriental Rugs & Carpets	*Meik & Ian McNaughton*
Making Period Dolls' House Accessories	*Andrea Barham*
Making Tudor Dolls' Houses	*Derek Rowbottom*
Making Victorian Dolls' House Furniture	*Patricia King*
Miniature Bobbin Lace	*Roz Snowden*
Miniature Embroidery for the Georgian Dolls' House	*Pamela Warner*
Miniature Embroidery for the Tudor and Stuart Dolls' House	
	Pamela Warner
Miniature Embroidery for the Victorian Dolls' House	*Pamela Warner*

Miniature Needlepoint Carpets	*Janet Granger*
More Miniature Oriental Rugs & Carpets	*Meik & Ian McNaughton*
Needlepoint 1/12 Scale: Design Collections for the Dolls' House	
	Felicity Price
New Ideas for Miniature Bobbin Lace	*Roz Snowden*
The Secrets of the Dolls' House Makers	*Jean Nisbett*

CRAFTS

American Patchwork Designs in Needlepoint	*Melanie Tacon*
A Beginners' Guide to Rubber Stamping	*Brenda Hunt*
Beginning Picture Marquetry	*Lawrence Threadgold*
Blackwork: A New Approach	*Brenda Day*
Celtic Cross Stitch Designs	*Carol Phillipson*
Celtic Knotwork Designs	*Sheila Sturrock*
Celtic Knotwork Handbook	*Sheila Sturrock*
Celtic Spirals and Other Designs	*Sheila Sturrock*
Complete Pyrography	*Stephen Poole*
Creative Backstitch	*Helen Hall*
Creative Embroidery Techniques Using Colour Through Gold	
	Daphne J. Ashby & Jackie Woolsey
The Creative Quilter: Techniques and Projects	*Pauline Brown*
Cross-Stitch Designs from China	*Carol Phillipson*
Decoration on Fabric: A Sourcebook of Ideas	*Pauline Brown*
Decorative Beaded Purses	*Enid Taylor*
Designing and Making Cards	*Glennis Gilruth*
Glass Engraving Pattern Book	*John Everett*
Glass Painting	*Emma Sedman*
Handcrafted Rugs	*Sandra Hardy*
How to Arrange Flowers: A Japanese Approach to English Design	
	Taeko Marvelly
How to Make First-Class Cards	*Debbie Brown*
An Introduction to Crewel Embroidery	*Mave Glenny*
Making and Using Working Drawings for Realistic Model Animals	
	Basil F. Fordham
Making Character Bears	*Valerie Tyler*
Making Decorative Screens	*Amanda Howes*
Making Fabergé-Style Eggs	*Denise Hopper*
Making Fairies and Fantastical Creatures	*Julie Sharp*
Making Greetings Cards for Beginners	*Pat Sutherland*
Making Hand-Sewn Boxes: Techniques and Projects	*Jackie Woolsey*
Making Knitwear Fit	*Pat Ashforth & Steve Plummer*
Making Mini Cards, Gift Tags & Invitations	*Glennis Gilruth*
Making Soft-Bodied Dough Characters	*Patricia Hughes*
Natural Ideas for Christmas: Fantastic Decorations to Make	
	Josie Cameron-Ashcroft & Carol Cox
New Ideas for Crochet: Stylish Projects for the Home	*Darsha Capaldi*
Papercraft Projects for Special Occasions	*Sine Chesterman*

GARDENING

PHOTOGRAPHY

ART TECHNIQUES

MAGAZINES

WOODTURNING ◆ WOODCARVING
FURNITURE & CABINETMAKING
THE ROUTER ◆ WOODWORKING
THE DOLLS' HOUSE MAGAZINE
OUTDOOR PHOTOGRAPHY
BLACK & WHITE PHOTOGRAPHY
MACHINE KNITTING NEWS
BUSINESSMATTERS

The above represents a full list of all titles currently published
or scheduled to be published.
All are available direct from the Publishers or through bookshops,
newsagents and specialist retailers.
To place an order, or to obtain a complete catalogue, contact:

**GMC Publications,
Castle Place, 166 High Street, Lewes,
East Sussex BN7 1XU,
United Kingdom
Tel: 01273 488005 Fax: 01273 478606
E-mail: pubs@thegmcgroup.com**

Orders by credit card are accepted